· THE ·
HUNGRY TRAVELER
MEXICO

· THE ·
HUNGRY TRAVELER
MEXICO

■

Marita Adair

Another idea by becker&mayer!, Ltd.

**Andrews McMeel
Publishing**
Kansas City

ISBN: 0-8362-2724-7
Library of Congress Catalog Card Number: 96-86643

This book is dedicated to
Guillermo Arias, my Mexican friend
who turned my timid eating ways into
adventurous ones fourteen years ago,
and to my friend Barbara Rodriguez,
for recruiting me to write this book.

· Contents ·

· *Diner's Advisory* ·

PEANUTS AND shellfish can be deadly to some people and sesame seeds and alcohol in food as well as other sauce ingredients can also cause serious dietary problems. If these foods are a concern there are precautions to take when dining in Mexico. It's best to avoid all moles if peanuts and sesame seeds, which are used abundantly in Mexican *mole* sauces, pose a problem. Other ingredients in the sauce that mask the aroma of peanuts and ground sesame seeds are imperceptible as well.

Many raw ceviche dishes may also contain seafood, such as shrimp or crab, which are toxic to people allergic to shellfish. Since the waiter may not know if the cook decides to toss in some shrimp into a ceviche cocktail billed as being made from fresh fish, it's best to avoid all ceviche if you have a shellfish allergy. If you're one who avoids alcohol, be aware that tequila, wine, and beer also figure into cooking sauces these days. Inclusion of these in a dish is usually mentioned as a featured ingredient on menus, but to be certain you may want to ask the waiter.

INTRODUCTION

· ∎ ·

Mᴇxɪᴄᴏ sɪᴍᴍᴇʀs with intriguing dishes. True south-of-the-border cuisine is an artful mix of Aztec, Mayan, Spanish, French, Italian, Lebanese, Austrian, French, English, and yes, United States foods and techniques—representing all the cultural influences imposed on this country in its more than three thousand–year history.

Mexico's rich storehouse of food goes back thousands of years and includes many gifts available to the Old World only after the Spanish Conquest of Mexico in 1519. These include avocado, sesame, peanuts, and chocolate. The Spaniards discovered a storehouse of delicious squash including chayote and chilacayote. Sweet potatoes and beans astounded the conquerors along with at least 100 varieties of chile. Exotic fruits found in Mexico prompted conquerors to describe them in letters home—the cherimoya, mamay, papaya, sapote, and guayaba—to name a few. They found new (to them) herbs and seasonings such as epazote and vanilla, and vegetables, or food used as vegetables, including corn, tomato, jícama, nopal cactus, and yucca. All of these, plus the turkey, the Spanish carried to Spain and introduced to the Old World after the conquest.

Today a new trend in Mexican cuisine features *alta cocina Mexicana* or high Mexican cuisine. The term, which appears frequently to describe refined Mexican cuisine, presents a new twist in food preparation. Extremely creative alta cocina chefs are coaxing new tastes from traditional foods and preparations combining them with European techniques: Pale mango sauce encircles a chocolate cream puff, pungent epazote is tamed into a brilliant fish sauce, maguey wrappers traditionally used for mixiotes (meat cooked in a sauce in a paper wrapper) engulf specially seasoned fish. Ground peanuts, usually used in mole, find new life as a sauce for beef. This is the latest phase for visitors to explore among Mexico's cuisines. However, be forewarned: any quest into the country's cuisine could begin a lifetime of travel.

Beyond Tex-Mex

Travelers expecting Mexico's foods to be like their local fast-food Mexican restaurant are in for a surprise—authentic Mexican cuisine is rarely found outside its borders. Combination plates, ordered by the number, food swimming in yellow cheese and runny beans, watered-down guacamole, and food sprinkled with sliced green or black olives and dollops of sour cream just isn't Mexican. Pinto beans are almost the only food to cross Mexico's borders with some semblance of the original. On the other hand, sizzling platters of fajitas are the one food that seems to have originated (or at least been perfected) in the United States and crossed south. Fajitas are fast becoming a Mexican menu staple especially in restaurants catering to U.S. visitors. However, if Tex-Mex food and crispy taco shells are your idea of Mexican food, get ready for many surprises—probably an abundance of satisfying ones.

From region to region and village to city an amazing assortment of dishes rises to tempt the palate. This book is intended to guide visitors through the labyrinth of Mexico's gastronomic choices and widen culinary horizons. With this book diners can confidently order meals in chrome-and-Formica-decorated restaurants, in market fondas, and in linen-and-silver-clad establishments.

As you travel, you'll discover that Mexico is a country without any shortage of restaurants, bakeries, and food markets. The country's varied cuisines take center stage in elegant fine-dining restaurants, cafés in jungle clearings, urban alleys, private homes, haciendas, mansions, and the open-air markets where food is authentic and tasty. Eating is such a visible part of the culture that on almost any short walk tastebuds begin exercising at the aroma of grilled onions and sizzling beef and pork tacos wafting streetside as pushcart cooks supply quick snacks to busy pedestrians. Others sell mangoes on a stick sculpted to hold the dripping juices, fresh and crunchy jícama peppered with chile and lime, and deep-fried pork skins dripping in fresh salsa or dribbled with fresh lime and ground chile. Outdoor village markets spill forth a plethora of exotic tropical fruits and vegetables, while the shelves of supermarkets and abarrotes (small neighborhood stores) showcase the basics of Mexico's food traditions in cans, jars, plastic, and cellophane.

Regional Food Generalities

Some food connoisseurs divide Mexico into five loosely formed regions—the Gulf Coast, Pacific Coast, northern and southern Mexico, and central Mexico, also called the Heartland. Loose generalities tie these different regions together: the Gulf Coast, encompassing the states of Tamaulipas, Veracruz, and Campeche, features seafood, tropical fruits, rich tamales, special sauces, and a Caribbean influence of black beans and fried bananas. The Pacific Coast states of Sinaloa, Nayarit, Jalisco, Guerrero, and Colima include much of the same foods but black beans are the norm south of Acapulco. Pozole traditions (a pork and hominy soup), and entirely different fish preparations take center stage on this coast. Baja California, also a part of this broad Pacific Coast region, boasts a prominent wine production and seafood. The Heartland, enveloping Mexico City and the states of México, Hidalgo, Puebla, Tlaxcala, Guanajuato, Michoacán, Morelos, Aguascalientes, and Querétaro, proffers cheese, wine,

English miner's fare, sweets, dozens of tamales, breads, and sauces. Puebla alone stands out as the mother of many of Mexico's cuisine scene stealers such as mole (a rich sauce), chiles en nogada (stuffed chiles), rompope (an eggnog-like drink), and mixiotes (meat steamed in a paper wrapper). The northern Mexico states of Coahuila, Nuevo León, Durango, and Zacatecas are known for cabrito (roast kid), charro beans (flavored pinto beans), and flour tortillas. Southern Mexico, encompassing the Yucatán Peninsula, Chiapas, Tabasco, and Oaxaca, offers some of Mexico's richest cuisine where cooks excel in the use of chiles, ground seeds, tamales, black beans, and sauce making. However, these broad divisions don't truly tell the story of Mexico's deeply complex and varied cuisines.

How This Book Is Organized

For the purposes of this book, rather than divide the food by region I've divided it alphabetically by food name in the Menu Primer A to Z, with cross-references for further explanation in Regional/Seasonal Specialties, Market Buying Tips, Comfort Foods, Beverages A to Z, and Useful Words Quick Reference Guide. To see how tacos, tamales, cheese, soup, chicken, and dozens of other foods vary from region to region or state to state, use the Menu Primer A to Z as a guide to finding variations in Regional/Seasonal Specialties. For tips on buying chiles, coffee, fresh fruit, packaged goods, and more, look in Market Buying Tips. Homesick for familiar food?

Find something familiar like chicken soup, sandwiches, oatmeal, and Cream of Wheat in Comfort Foods. Drinks of all kinds are listed in Beverages A to Z. The section called Useful Words Quick Reference Guide will take you quickly to the basic dining words for salt, pepper, fork, glass, cup, etc.—words you may need but don't know in Spanish.

The Big Four Tourist Getters— Fruit, Vegetables, Ice, and Water

Most guides to Mexico recommend eating only peeled fruit, cooked vegetables, and cooked seafood, drinking only purified water, and avoiding ice (which may be made with unpurified water). All are excellent recommendations. Fruit that can't be peeled and uncooked vegetables and raw seafood used in ceviche (uncooked, marinated fish and seafood) may have been washed in unclean or unpurified water, or worse, not washed at all. However, better restaurants catering to tourists take the necessary precautions to make sure their fruits and vegetables are clean. And bottled, purified water is available everywhere. Raw seafood is iffy under even the best circumstances.

On the other hand, so much has been written about not eating fruits and vegetables because of the possibility of traveler's diarrhea, called "Montezuma's revenge" in Mexico, that tourists are often overly cautious. Because of it they don't really explore and discover the rich variety of Mexican food. This overly cautious mind-set may also cause the opposite of diarrhea to occur. In fact constipation may be more common than diarrhea. This unspeakable affliction is seldom discussed since the malady rarely keeps anyone shut in the hotel room the way diarrhea can. To avoid the constipation problem, try to strike a balance in food selection. Fresh fruit salads are easily found. Plus, a fine fresh salad bar in a good restaurant, or a hot soup with plenty of vegetables, may be just the ticket to keeping things in proper working order.

Restaurants by Any Other Name

The Spanish word for restaurant is *restaurante* (res tah RAHN teh). When inquiring about a restaurant the Spanish word is used. But many restaurants use the English word in their official names, even restaurants with a totally Mexican clientele. Other words, however, also announce eating establishments. For example, fonda, cenaduria, café, mesón, hostería, and cafetería, are the most prominent names used besides restaurant.

A *fonda* (FOHN dah) can refer to a restaurant in a market, or a streetside restaurant specializing in Mexican food.

A *cenaduría* is open only for dinner—*cena* (CEH nah)—and usually showcases regional food.

A *café* (kah FEH) may be a small, cozy place, or a large dining hall.

Mesón (meh SOHN) and hostería (ohs teh REE ah) once referred to places where people stabled their livestock while traveling and where they could also sleep and get a meal. Nowadays a mesón or hostería may be a restaurant only or the word may designate a hotel as well.

A *cafetería* (kah feh teh REE ah) is seldom like a cafeteria in the United States where diners move along in a line with a tray and plate selecting food that's tallied by a cashier at the end. Instead, a cafetería is simply another word for restaurant. Hotels often advertise *"servicio de cafetería"* (sehr BEE see oh deh kah feh teh REE ah) to designate their casual coffee shop–style restaurant. A fine dining restaurant in a hotel will have a separate name.

Bars and Cantinas

Bar is the word assigned to a place for drinks, and the English designation of "lobby bar" is commonly used in Mexican hotels. A *cantina* (kan TEE nah), however, is usually another sort of place entirely. If it's in a hotel, or part of a nice restaurant, the word means bar. But if "Cantina" is emblazoned above a place facing the street with swinging doors at the entrance, then the territory inside may have many personalities. Typically cantinas are men-only places (though by law women are allowed), where heavy drinking is the order of the day and where fights aren't uncommon. The aroma of stale beer mixed with even staler cigarette smoke often wafts out to the street, and a trio may be heard playing to men who sing along off tune. Free *botanas*, or appetizers, many of which are delicious, often accompany drinks in cantinas. Most cantinas, however, are guarded territories of the locals where foreigners are observed warily. A few middle-class to upscale cantinas in Mexico City are great, friendly places for male and female foreigners to comfortably eat and drink without concern for barroom brawls. However, a woman alone in a cantina may attract persistent, unwanted, and unpleasant attention. Foreigners wishing to explore cantina life should consider doing so in the early afternoon, before drunkenness overwhelms the regulars and before foreigners may become viewed as fight-worthy.

Market Meals

A lot of foreigners really enjoy Mexico's market food since these market fondas provide the venue for tasting regional foods that restaurants may not offer. Markets are some of the best places for sampling well-seasoned, authentic Mexican food at bargain prices.

The main drawback to dining in a market may be the lack of hygienic procedures in some places. Tap water, or water hauled in by the bucketful from a communal tap, won't be purified, and it's used for all cooking and washing purposes. (But it's important to add that used wash water is never used for cooking water.) Dishes and utensils may be washed in cold, well-used water. Even if the dishwater is changed frequently, hot water is almost never available. And finally the cook may also be the cashier, handling both food and money with the same un-washed hands.

Having said all of that, there are ways to get around the hygiene problem if you're game. Look for a market fonda serving food on disposable plates and using disposable utensils and cups. Many use a plastic reusable plate with a clean square of utility paper on top. Food, such as barbacoa, tacos, and tamales, are placed on the paper relieving the worry about how the plate was previously washed. These are the fondas to choose.

And there are other ways to enjoy market food with an eye toward proper hygiene. One is to order only finger foods such as tacos, barbacoa, or tamales. Another is to arrive early in the day when the food is freshly prepared and hot. Carry your own plastic bowl or plate, fork, and spoon. It's not unheard of for foreigners to provide their own straws and spoons or forks—so why not a bowl or plate if that's a concern. These can be purchased easily in Mexico. Don't drink from a glass. Instead, carry straws to drink from cans or bottles. Yes, market people may snicker at all of these precautions, but what do you care. Select a clean-looking, neatly kept restaurant. One that has clients likely means the food is good. Watch to see how money and food are handled.

Needless to say microwave ovens aren't a fixture in market food stalls. Request hot food by saying *"bien caliente"* (bee YEHN kahl eeh EN teh), and emphasize it so that you get a very hot meal.

Washing hands before a meal in a market may introduce the bucket, cup, and laundry detergent ritual. A bucket of clear, cold water sits beside a sink that drains but has no running water. First you dip the cup in the water, and wet your hands. Then pinch a bit of detergent grains from the provided container and lather. Rinse with the rest of the cup of water and dry your hands on your clothes.

Dining Hours and Customs

Desayuno (deh sih OOH noh)—Breakfast. Breakfast is generally available until the Mexican lunch hour begins between 1 P.M. and 2 P.M. In fact, to anyone seated for lunch at 11 or 11:30 A.M. or even noon, the waiter will probably present the breakfast menu since a Mexican would never consider eating lunch so early. Mexicans eat a light breakfast at home of perhaps a piece of sweet bread, fruit, and *atole* (a sweet, warm drink) or coffee and that *may* be it until lunch, with perhaps some nibbles in between. Travelers can create their own breakfast and avoid restaurants altogether. A simple pastry-and-fruit desayuno is easy to assemble from fresh-baked sweet bread *(pan dulce)* and market-bought fruit. In a restaurant, there's a wide breakfast selection that can be a Mexican-style breakfast with spicy eggs and tortillas, or a lunch-like feast with a big steak or beef stew. But it's a cinch to find American-style breakfast food such as pancakes and cereal (usually corn flakes), or bacon and eggs and toast prepared many ways.

Almuerzo (ahl MWEHR soh)—Brunch. After a light breakfast so early and the Mexican lunch so late (at 3 or 3:30), it's no surprise that Mexicans created something in between—almuerzo—the bridge between breakfast and lunch. Many restaurants fill up mid-morning for this brunch when diners order a breakfast so hearty (eggs and steak, stew, caldo, etc.) that it could easily be lunch. At this time patrons will be asked "*¿Va a almorzar?*" (bah ah ahl mohr SAHR) meaning "Would you like almuerzo?" There's no separate almuerzo menu, so whatever menu is presented will more than likely have both traditional breakfasts with eggs as well as more substantial ones with chilaquiles, steak, etc.

Comida (koh MEE dah)—Lunch. Most restaurants are prepared to provide lunch beginning around 12:30 P.M., but everything will be truly ready around 1 or 1:30 P.M. which is the starting time for the Mexican lunch hour, traditionally the largest meal of the day. Those preferring to dine without a crowd, and with more attentive service, will want to target the early portion of the mealtime. Mexicans take from two to three hours for lunch. By 3 or 3:30 P.M. restaurant waiters swirl around tables filled with Mexicans during their preferred lunch time; the crowd will remain heavy until around 5 P.M. when workers head back to the office and work until 7 or 8 P.M.

Some of the best Mexican food is served during the *comida corrida* (koh MEE dah koh RREE dah) hours of 1:30 or 2 to 4 P.M. Diners wishing to indulge themselves earlier may be told the food isn't ready. Like a blue-plate special, the comida corrida is the restaurant's home-style special meal of the day. The steady lineup of food goes like this: An appetizer of perhaps fresh fruit or homemade soup or both is followed by a plate of seasoned or plain rice, then the main meat course, which may include beans and a small salad on the same plate. Although the practice of asking that the rice course be served with the main course goes against Mexican dining tradition, for foreigners it often makes the main course of a comida corrida more interesting, going well with the light sauce that often accompanies a main course such as *lomo adobado* (pork loin in a savory chile sauce) or *albóndigas* (meatballs in a delicious-but-thin brown sauce). Waiters and waitresses generally will comply with that request without hesitation.

It's all topped off by a choice of coffee or a small dessert such as flan (a delicious egg custard), gelatin, or a scoop of ice cream. A cup of coffee or tea is usually included, but a cold drink with the meal usually costs extra. The comida corrida is of the home-cooking genre and is a good time to sample wholesome food such as Mexicans enjoy at home. It's the closest thing to market food, which is some of the best fare. Once a generous feast, however, the comida corrida, generally speaking, is experiencing "downsizing," though it can still be filling. Soup is served in smaller bowls than previously. Meat and salad portions are smaller than in the past. A beverage often costs extra and dessert is disappearing.

Merienda (meh ree YEHN dah)—*Botana* and Drink Time. The merienda bridges the gap between lunch and the dinner hour, around 9 or 10 P.M. Merienda, served between 5 or 6 and 8 P.M., is a time for tea, coffee, or alcoholic drinks and botanas (snacks). Cafés and coffeehouses fill up for this custom, though the practice is not very often heralded by name—locals just know what they are doing. Many fashionable hotel lobby bars, especially in Mexico City, have turned the merienda into the Mexican equivalent of the British high tea, serving scrumptious French-style pastries and bite-size Mexican botanas.

Cena (SEH nah)—Dinner. A typical Mexican cena at home is a light meal served around 9 or 10 P.M. However, restaurants are prepared to serve both light and heavy meals during the dinner hour, so you'll never lack for choices.

The equivalent of "Enjoy your meal" in Mexico is *"Buen provecho"* (bwain pro BEH cho). The waiter may offer this phrase when everyone has been served. On other occasions, guests wait for the host to say it before beginning the meal.

Table Settings

The normal table settings prevail in Mexico. But if something is missing it's handy to know the proper word for the object. There's no need to memorize a phrase, just say the word with a question in your voice and the waiter will usually understand. For a list of these terms and others in English, see Useful Words Quick Reference Guide at the end of the book.

Reading the Menu and Ordering

Cartas (KAHR tahs) or menus have several words to designate hors d'oeuvres including botana, antojitos, entremeses, and entrada. But the waiter may say, "*¿Algo para empezar?*" (AHL goh PAH rah em peh SAHR) meaning "Would you like an appetizer?" Literally translated it means "Would you like something to start?"

For a main course the waiter may ask, "*¿Para plato fuerte?*" (PAH rah PLAH toh FWEHR teh). Literally, this means "for the strong plate," but he's asking for an entree preference. The term plato fuerte doesn't appear on menus. Instead main courses may be listed as fish, seafood, chicken, etc., or entrees may be headed with the word *especialidades* (ehs peh cee ahl ee DAH dehs), meaning "specialties," followed by particular food divisions.

A section of the menu may be headed "Bebidas" (beh BEEH dah), which means drinks, followed by what's offered. The waiter may ask, "*¿Para beber?*" (PAH rah beh BEHR), meaning "What'll you have to drink?" More often the question is phrased "*¿Para tomar?*" (PAH rah toh MAHR). The word for an alcoholic drink is *alcólico* (ahl KOH lee koh) and for soft drink, *refresco* (REH FREHS koh).

The usual word for dessert is *postre* (POHS treh). The waiter may ask, "*¿Para postre?*" (PAH rah POHS treh) as a way of saying, "What will you have for dessert?"

How Hot Is It?

Mexican menus don't come with a heat-factor rating for individual foods, so you have to pursue this topic on your own. Despite taking the precaution of asking, you may still take an unexpected venture into a spicy blaze. If so, soften the effect by eating bread, tortillas, or chips, or even drinking milk.

There's some comfort in knowing that most spicy heat comes from salsas, and fresh chiles that are set on the table and which diners add according to their personal *picante* tolerance. Some foods, however, such as mole, *sopa xochitl* (with fresh serrano peppers), and some cooked sauces arrive with the heat cooked in. In defense of mole, I should add that the heat quotient varies and some are quite mild. (For how to ask if something is picante [spicy hot], see also Useful Words Quick Reference Guide *Spicy Hot*.)

Cultural Pointers for Ordering and Dining

Most meals will flow smoothly, served as they should be by attentive waiters. There are, however, odd (to foreigners) intricacies in ordering and obtaining the bill which *can* occur and which are mentioned below. The most important thing to remember is that foreigners as a group tend to rush through meals, and fail to adopt the more leisurely Mexican pace which truly allows for enjoying the experience.

Sitting down to order may not be as forthright as it first appears. Efficient waiters may be so eager to take the order that foreigners aren't given sufficient time to digest the menu. If you need more time, indicate it by holding your thumb and index finger almost together—and smile. This is the Mexican way of gesturing, "Give me a minute—please." The waiter will oblige instantly. However, asking a waiter to return can be the equivalent of sending him to Patagonia. He gets busy, forgets, starts chatting with the other waiters with his back to the room, or gives the lollygagging diners more than *plenty* of time. "Where's the waiter?" is an oft-heard expression.

When you're ready to order, the one thing *not* to do is summon the waiter by wiggling an index finger. In Mexico that's demeaning. While the waiter has probably been around foreigners enough to know this is a forgivable cultural difference between the diner and him, he still looses face if he responds. He might arrive at your table despite the social blunder, but he may be somber, stiff, and formal. What to do? Beckon the waiter the Mexican way. Cup the fingers together rigidly, with the palm in a scoop as if to hold a fragile bird egg. Then move your hand, palm side down, in a downward motion toward your body or inward to the chest. This is the accepted "come here" motion in Mexico. Or you can make the "sheet" sound with your mouth followed by the "come here" movement of your cupped hand. Strange as it seems, the Mexican equivalent of the somewhat annoying American "pssst" is a widely used and acceptable attention-getting noise that can bring a waiter running. To create the sound, hold your teeth together, and blow through them while saying "sheet," with a nearly silent "t." It won't sound like "sheet" exactly but it's not supposed to—it's a noise.

After the meal arrives, the waiter may hover too much or not enough—there's seldom a middle ground. A hovering waiter is eager to whisk your plate away if you pause between bites. A nonhovering waiter fails to refill glasses, replenish the butter, or ask if you need anything. "Sheet" is useful then. Oddly, waiter training often doesn't include surveying neighboring tables for deficiencies. Thus, they deadhead straight to a summoning table without looking left or right. "Sheet" is about all you can do in that case.

Single diners will be less well served over all than those dining in a group.

You'll seldom feel rushed through a meal in Mexico by having the check thrust at you upon arrival of your entree. It's one of the country's most gracious customs. Only a few restaurants in Mexico City will present a bill when the food is served, and then it's only as a service to busy patrons; everybody in the capital knows an unrequested check at those restaurants isn't a hint to vacate the table. Normally you request the bill—after you've stayed as long as you want. To request it say, *"La cuenta por favor"* (lah KWEN tah pohr fah BOR), which means, "The check please." Presenting the bill only on request is such an entrenched custom that waiters will wait patiently for your exit rather than mention you've stayed long past closing, or even hint that a line of people is waiting to be seated. On the other hand, if you're in a rush, ask for the check when your meal arrives. Your server may not think you really mean it—after all no one in Mexico eats in a mad dash like that—so several reminders may have to follow your initial request. Too, waiters can disappear so completely that diners have been known to hunt them down in the kitchen.

And finally, waiters and waitresses in Mexico don't introduce themselves and announce that they're your server, so diners may be at a loss as to what to call the person waiting on them. It isn't the norm to call the person waiter or waitress, which is *mesero* (meh SEH roh) or *mesera* (meh SEH rah). Instead use *joven* (HOH ven) for a young man, *señor* (sen YOHR), for an older man, and *señorita* (sen yoh REE tah), which means miss, for a woman regardless of her age or her marital status. These are polite ways of addressing someone as sir or miss.

And finally there's the subject of leftovers. It seems like a pity to let a perfectly good portion of meat be carried off to the trash when it would make a good lunch tomorrow, but Mexican dining etiquette doesn't permit bagging leftovers to take

home. Don't even ask for a carry-home container—
it's really bad form—because you'll make Americans look gauche in the eyes of the natives. Having laid down that law, there may be an exception.
If you're discreet, and dining in a chrome and
Formica-decorated restaurant, something easily
portable can be stuffed into a plastic bag that you've
brought along. Just don't ask the establishment to
do this for you.

Of Tips and Taxes,
Hidden Costs, and Receipts

There's a 12 to 17 percent value added tax, called
IVA, in Mexico. It varies depending on where you
are. Presently the 12 percent tax applies in Cancún,
Cozumel, and Southern Baja California, while 17
percent is added elsewhere.

Generally speaking, IVA, or *impuesto* (eem PWEHS
toh), is included in the cost appearing on the menu.
(It was once required by law to be included in posted
prices, but that's no longer true.) To be sure if tax is
included, scan the fine print at the bottom of the
menu where the notice about taxes usually appears.
Most restaurants don't include the tip, called *propina*
(pro PEE nah), when the bill is presented, but some
places do.

Then there's the matter of the *cubierto* (koo bee
EHR toh) or cover charge for table condiments.
Those delicious rolls and butter or perhaps pâté and
marinated vegetables placed on the table after you've

ordered may not be free. Usually there's no charge for rolls and butter, or even the pickled vegetables, but when there is, only a few restaurants mention it in the menu's fine print. Thus, the cubierto charge may be a surprise when the bill arrives. Sometimes the cubierto is a nominal charge, of one dollar or so, but it can also be rather steep.

Figure the tip *before tax* as 10 percent of the price of the meal in ordinary restaurants and 15 percent in fine restaurants. If the menu price already includes tax (and it usually does), then the general rule is to tip 10 percent on the total. It's a sort of average that's easy to do without hovering over a calculator to separate out the tax. Truly fine service should garner a 20 percent tip in a nice restaurant. Occasionally a waiter in a fine restaurant may express displeasure at a tip that's not on top of the tax. A waiter's tip disappointment is registered with a long look at the tip followed by a harump, raised brows, negative head shaking, or even a scowl. In that case it's wise to ponder in whose pocket (yours or the waiter's) the money should best remain.

If you need a receipt for tax purposes or your expense account, it may take some real effort. A few years ago the government cracked down on tax-deductible meals (for Mexican citizens) and began requiring the presentation of a special card, called a *registro* (reh HEES troh), to obtain a receipt. So if you ask for a receipt called a *recibo* (reh SEE boh) or a *nota de consumo* (NOH tah deh kohn SOOM oh), you'll be asked for your registro. Just say you want a *comanda* (koh MAHN dah), which is a general term for a pad of generic receipts that most restaurants have.

Buen Provecho!

MENU PRIMER A TO Z
(SPANISH TO ENGLISH)

· ■ ·

THIS SECTION provides the most important basics in menu reading. From here the reader is referred to more specific sections for detailed information on regional preparations, beverages, comfort foods, tips on buying food, pottery, and kitchen utensils in open-air markets and more traditional stores, and to useful words in English with their Spanish translation.

Abulón (ah boo LOHN). Abalone.

Aceite (ah SEH TEH). Oil. This is usually *aceite vegetal* (ah SEH teh beh heh TAHL) or vegetable oil. Olive oil isn't often offered in Mexican restaurants as a dressing although it's used in cooking. *Aceite de olivo* (ah SEH teh deh oh LEE boh) is olive oil. (See also *Aderezo* below.)

Acelgas (ah SEHL gahs). Swiss chard. Usually acelgas is used in a soup devoted to it called *sopa de acelgas* (SOH pah day ah SEHL gahs).

Aceituna (ah seh TOOH nah). Olive. Olives are called aceituna, while the tree is called *olivo* (oh LEE boh). Olive oil is *aceite de olivo* (ah SEH teh deh oh LEE boh).

Olive cultivation arrived in Mexico after the Spanish Conquest, but was soon forbidden because of its potential for competition with the Spanish olive industry. Portions of the crop survived, however, and olive plantations can be found in the states of Jalisco, Hidalgo, Guanajuato, Querétaro, Coahuila, Chihuahua, Baja California, Aguascalientes, Morelos, and near Xochimilco, south of Mexico City. Xochi-milco hosts an olive and amaranth fair each February.

Achiote (ah chee OH teh). The dark red seed of the annatto tree. (Besides those listed below, see also *Cochinita (Pibil), Pollo (Pibil), Tik-n-xik*, and Market Buying Tips: *Achiote/Achiote Preparado*.)

• *Achiote preparado/recado de achiote/Recado rojo* (ah chee OH teh preh pah RAH doh/reh KAH doh deh ah chee OH teh/reh KAH do ROH hoh). Prepared achiote or achiote recipe. Either way this means ground achiote seed mixed into a harmonious paste with crushed garlic, oregano, cumin, and other spices to use as a luscious marinade for chicken and fish.

Acitrón (ah cee TROHN). Candied biznaga (organ) cactus. Sold widely in Mexico, it's used in sweet tamales and in meat fillings.

Acuyo (ah KOO yoh). An aromatic leaf used in cooking.

Aderezo (ah deh REH soh). Salad dressing. Seldom will you encounter standard dressings such as ranch or *rancho* (RAHN cho), Thousand island or *mil isla* (meel EES lah), French or *Francés* (frahn SEHS). Salads are usually served with a wedge of lime for flavor. Often, the restaurant will offer vinegar and oil as an afterthought. If you want vinegar and oil, ask for *vinagre y aceite* (beeh NAH greh eeh ah SEH teh). More sophisticated restaurants, however, may offer a vinaigrette or *vinagreta* (veen ah GREH tah) or some other house dressing called *aderezo de la casa* (ah deh REH soh deh la KAH sah).

Adobo (ah DOH boh). A savory paste for seasoning meat. The paste, made of freshly ground chiles, herbs, spices, tomatoes, and often vinegar or the juice of fresh oranges, is used two ways: If it's spread on grilling meat, the dish is called *carne adobado* (KAHR neh ah DOH boh), meaning grilled meat flavored with adobo; *en adobo* (ehn ah DOH boh) refers to the sauce formed by the paste ingredients when they're cooked with oven-roasted meat or in a stove-top meaty brew. Adobo generally is not *picante* (pee KAHN teh), that is, fiery hot to the taste, but to a foreigner's tongue the predominant flavor of an oven or stove-top adobo mixture may taste as if the cook went a little heavy on the chile powder. You never know precisely how something with adobo will taste, but it's almost always worth trying. A side order of rice is often just the thing to cut the heavy chile flavor enough for pure enjoyment of the dish. (See also Market Buying Tips: *Adobo*.)

Agrio/Agria (AHG gree yoh, AH gree yah). Sour.

Aguacate (ahg wah KAH teh). Avocado. This native fruit is the prime ingredient of guacamole salad. Diced avocado also adds a richness to Mexican vegetable soups and to green salsa.

Aguas Frescas (AHG wahs FREHS kahs). Fresh fruit-flavored water. (See also *Agua Frescas* entries in Beverages A to Z and Market Buying Tips.)

Ahumada (ah ooh MAH dah). Smoked.

Ajillo (ah HEE yoh). A mild red cooking sauce created by melding garlic and roasted red chiles.

Ajo (AH hoh). Garlic.

A La (ah lah). A regional or city style or way of fixing something. A la Poblano would be the way a dish is prepared in the state of Puebla. (See also *Estilo* below.)

Albahaca (ahl bah HAH kah). Basil.

Albóndigas (ahl BOHN dee gahs). Meatballs. Always tasty, but rarely more than two small- to medium-sized meatballs come on a dinner-size plate surrounded by more deliciously smooth brown meat sauce than the meatballs can absorb. Order rice with it and you're set for a meal.

Albondigón (ahl bohn dee GOHN). Meat loaf.

Alcaparras (ahl kah PAH rahs). Capers.

Alchofa (ahl CHO fah). Artichoke.

Al Gusto (ahl GOOS toh). Something al gusto will be prepared the way you like it. Seafood especially will be offered al gusto, usually with a choice of being fried in butter, or with fresh garlic, or prepared in a tomato sauce. You'll see al gusto used with eggs as well.

Almeja (ahl MEH hah). Clam.

Almendra (ahl MEHN drah). Almond.

Al Mojo de Ajo (ahl MOH hoh deh AH hoh). Garlic cloves. Garlic-flavored seafood is usually referred to as *al mojo de ajo* (ahl MOH hoh deh AH hoh), meaning lots of chopped garlic is used in the preparation. (See also *Ajo* above.)

Alubia (ah LOO bee yah). A small white bean used in soup.

Amaranto (ah mah RAHN toh). Amaranth. A pre-Conquest grain, it's finding new uses in modern Mexico. Alta cocina Mexican chefs are using the fine flour form of it, mixed with finely ground brown sugar, as a dusting for pastries. (See also Market Buying Tips: *Amaranto* and *Alegría*.)

Ancas de Rana (AHN kahs deh RAH nah). Frog's legs.

Ancho (AHN cho). A dried chile. (See also *Chiles Seco* below.)

Anchoa (ahn CHO ah). Anchovy.

Añejo (ahn YEH hoh). Aged. The word is used to describe certain cheeses, beef, and tequila.

Angulas (ahn GOO lahs). Baby eels. (See also *Antojitos* below.)

Annatto (ahn NAH toh). A tree producing tiny red seeds called achiote. Ground achiote makes a mild spice used as flavoring and coloring. The spice is used in preparing chicken and pork pibil, on fish, and in various meat preparations in the Yucatán. (See also *Achiote Preparado* above.)

Antojitos (ahn toh HEE tohs). Literally "little whims," known as appetizers. On menus they appear in two categories: *Botanas* (boh TAH nahs) are small portions usually of Mexican specialties and are sometimes served free with drinks; *Antojitos* or Mexican specialties called *especialidades mexicanos* (ehs pehs cee ah lee DAH dehs MEH hee KAH nohs) may be a small portion or a full-sized meal and therefore too large to think of as a snack preceding a full meal. Its placement on the menu—with appetizers, or further on with entrees, will generally give you an idea of whether it's sized as a snack or as a filling entree. Although they have different names, many appetizers are so similar that it's difficult to tell them apart. (Besides those listed below, see also Regional/Seasonal Specialties: *Botanas*.)

- *Angulas* (ahn GOO lahs). Imported canned baby eels. The custom for serving this expensive appetizer comes from Spain.
- *Sope* (SOH peh). A spread of refried beans, cheese, bits of meat, tomato, and crumbled cheese atop a fried cornmeal (masa) patty. The sope has many variations.
- *Tlacoyo* (tlah KOH yoh). A canoe-shaped cornmeal (masa) appetizer of pre-Hispanic origin. Sometimes cooked beans are mashed into the dough before it's fried. Green or red sauces are ladled on and the whole tlacoyo is topped with chopped onions, crumbled cheese, or sour cream.
- *Tostada* (tohs TAH dah). A fried corn tortilla

topped with beans, shredded lettuce, tomato, chicken, and cheese. The large tostada appears countrywide. As a botana or antojito it is a miniature version of the large dinner-size tostada.

Apio (AH pee yoh). Celery.

Arenques (ah REHN kehs). Herring.

Armadillo (ahr mah DEE yoh). Armadillo. Restaurants focusing on pre-Conquest food will serve this curious animal whose red meat tastes like roast beef. Were it not for the custom of serving the feet along with the leg portion, diners could avoid acknowledging the little critter.

Arroz (ah RROHS). Rice. Rice is generally prepared for main courses two ways. On menus both kinds appear under soup and are known as *sopa seca* (SOH pah SAY kah) or dry soup—but they aren't soups. (Besides those listed below, see also Regional/Seasonal Specialties: *Arroz*.)

- *Arroz blanco* (ah RROHS BLAHN koh). White rice.
- *Arroz con leche* (ah RROHS kohn LEH cheh). A dessert rice pudding flavored with sugar and cinnamon.
- *Arroz a la Mexicana* (ah RROHS ah lah meh hee KAH nah). Mexican rice. It may be colored red with a spice such as achiote or saffron and dap-

pled with peas. Or it may be more elaborate, cooked in a tomato broth with peas, onions, and chopped carrots.

Asadero (ah sah DEH roh). A white, mozzarella-like cheese used in quesadillas. (See also *Queso*, Regional / Seasonal Specialties and Market Buying Tips.)

Asado /Asada (ah SAH doh /ah SAH dah). Meat that is either broiled, grilled, or charbroiled.

Ate (AH teh). Staggeringly sweet candied fruit paste served as a dessert accompanied by sliced white cheese. (See also *Dulce* below.)

Atún (ah TOON). Tuna.

Avena (ah BEH nah). Oatmeal. A breakfast staple. The oatmeal will arrive swimming in milk unless you ask for milk to be served on the side in a pitcher or glass.

Aves (AH BEHS). Fowl or poultry. This is the heading for poultry on a menu.

Azafrán (ah sah FRAHN). Saffron.

Azúcar (ah SOO kahr). Sugar. Christopher Columbus brought sugar cultivation to the Dominican Republic, but the Mexican conqueror Hernán Cortés introduced it to Mexico. He cultivated it on his enormous land grants near Cuernavaca, in the state of Morelos, where sugarcane is still grown. Besides Morelos, an enormous agricultural business transforms the green stalky plant into table sugar in the states of Veracruz, Tamaulipas, Sinaloa, and Jalisco. Low-calorie sugar may be offered at a few top restaurants, but the brand may be Mexican.

Bacalao (bah kah LAH oh). Cod. Mexicans seem to like dried cod and find uses for it in numerous dishes all of which smell very fishy.

Bagre (BAH greh). Catfish.

Barbacoa (bahr bah KOH ah). Barbecue. Mexican-style barbecue bears no resemblance to its north-of-the-border namesake. The Mexican barbacoa potpourri artfully teams a whole lamb, goat, rabbit, or chicken, with chiles, epazote, onions, potatoes, carrots, cabbage, and garbanzo beans, all baked in the ground in a bed of roasted maguey leaves. Or it may be made more simply with a chile sauce. Either way the result is delicious fork-tender meat with no overwhelming chile taste. It may also be steamed in the oven. Green and red sauces are served at the table for flavor.

On weekends, especially, you'll see barbacoa signs while traveling through the countryside in most of Mexico, and it's worth a stop just to savor the uniqueness of this culinary treat. The Yucatecan pit-baked barbacoa is cochinta or pollo pibil, but the achiote sauce is completely different and both are baked in banana leaves. (See also *Achiote* above and *Cochinta* and *Pollo* below, and Regional/Seasonal Specialties: *Barbacoa*.)

Bebida/Bebidas (beh BEE dah/beh BEE dahs). Drink/drinks. This is the beverage section heading on most menus. (See also Beverages A to Z.)

Berenjena (beh rehn HEH nah). Eggplant.

Berro (BEH rroh). Watercress.

Betabel (beh tah BEHL). Beets.

Bif (beef). Beef. The Spaniards introduced cattle or *vacas* (BAH kahs) to Mexico. Meat of the cow is also referred to as *carne de res* (KAHR neh deh rehs) or carne de vaca (KAHR neh deh BAH kah). A steak is *bifstek* (BEEF stehk) or bistek (BEE stehk). (See also Useful Words Quick Reference Guide for proper terms for well done, medium rare, etc.)

Birria (BEER ree yah). Lamb, goat, pork, or veal marinated and steam-baked in a delicious red sauce. Because it's served in a bowl surrounded by a rich red broth, it looks like soup, but it isn't considered a soup by Mexicans. When it isn't grandly announced by a special notice on the door, wall, or menu, it's usually listed under meats. A *birreria* (bee rehr REE ah) is a restaurant specializing in birria. (See also Regional/Seasonal Specialties: *Birria*.)

Blanco (BLAHN koh). White. The waiter may use this word to tell you the color of a sauce, soup, or other dish.

Bocoles (boh KOH lehs). Cornmeal masa stuffed with sausage, cheese, and chorizo—a specialty of San Luis Potosí. (See also Regional/Seasonal Specialties: *Botana*.)

Bolillo (boh LEE yoh). A large French-style roll. Baskets of this large fresh roll are served with most meals.

Along with many bakery goods in Mexico today the bolillo is the result of the French occupation of Mexico (1864–67). Napoleon III of France ensconced (with the help of a few high-placed Mexicans) his thirty-two-year-old Austrian cousin archduke Maximilian of Hapsburg and Maximilian's twenty-four-year-old wife Carlota in Mexico City as emperor and empress of Mexico. This began the mingling of yet other cuisines with those of Mexico. With them came Austrian and French techniques and specialties, which are still very prevalent today, especially in the country's breads and pastries.

Bolos de Masa (BOH lohs deh MAH sah). Shark meat–flavored cornmeal masa. (See also Regional/Seasonal Specialties: *Cazón*.)

Borracho (boh RRAH cho). Literally borracho means "drunk." In food it refers to the use of beer, wine, tequila, or other liquor in the preparation of a dish. *Frijoles borrachos* (drunken beans), for example, are flavored with beer.

Borrego (boh RREH goh). Lamb. Lamb roasted over wood coals is a delicious weekend countryside specialty in many parts of Mexico, especially in the state of Jalisco. It's accompanied by charro beans and tortillas. *Carnero* (kahr NEH roh) and *cordero* (kohr DEH roh) are other words for lamb. (See also Regional/Seasonal Specialties: *Borrego*.)

Botanas (boh TAH nah). Appetizers. (See also *Antojitos* above and Regional/Seasonal Specialties: *Botana*.)

Brazo de Reina (BRAH soh deh REH nah). A large Yucatecan tamal. (See also Regional/Seasonal Specialties: *Tamales*.)

Brocheta (broh CHEH tah). Shish kebab.

Brócoli (BROH koh lee). Broccoli.

Bruselas (BROO SEH lahs). Brussels sprouts.

Budín (booh DEEN). Pudding.

Buñuelo (boon WEH loh). A fried tortilla-size fritter glittered with sugar and cinnamon that's usually paired with hot chocolate or atole. In the United States a buñuelo is often called a *sopapilla* (soh pah PEE yah), but it's not known by that name in Mexico.

Burrito (BOOR ree toh). Any combination of beans, meat, and cheese rolled up in an oversized, soft wheat flour tortilla. It's offered more in northern Mexico than other parts of the country and it may come smothered in a chile sauce. A burrito dropped into a deep-fat fryer is transformed into a chimichanga, which is often topped with sour cream and guacamole or sliced avocado Chimichangas are found more in the United States than in Mexico. A taco is smaller than a burrito and is offered with a variety of tortillas and wider choice of fillings.

Cabrito (kah BREE toh). A milk-fed kid goat, rubbed with butter or oil, seasoned with salt, pepper, and lime, and roasted whole on a spit. A specialty of northern Mexico, the optimal weight for cabrito is eighteen pounds, but old goats can, and do, find their way to the table. The leg portion is a meatier choice than the rib portion. The latter may have more fat than meat clinging to the bones. (See also *Fritada* below, and Regional/Seasonal Specialties: *Cabrito*.)

Cacahuate (kah kah WAH teh). Peanut.

Cacao (kah KAH oh). Chocolate. (See also *Chocolate* below.)

Cajeta (kah HEH tah). Ordinarily, this means sweetened carmelized goat's or cow's milk. Goat's or cow's milk cajeta is delicious, and is often served as a haute cuisine crepe filling, as a filling for churros, and as an ice cream flavor. But why wait—scoop it from the jar and spread it on toast or a big warm roll. In some places cajeta may be something completely different—a marvelous invention of ground nuts, and fresh slices of the fruit such as mango, peach, etc., cooked with vanilla and sugar to a thick mixture. (See also Market Buying Tips: *Cajeta*.)

Calabaza (cah lah BAHS ah). Squash.

Calamar/Calamares (kah lah MAHR/kah lah MAH rehs). Squid.

Calamares en su Tinta (kah lah MAH rehs en sooh TEEN tah). Squid in its ink or juice.

Caldo (KAHL doh). A meat broth. Rarely is anything so simple as a broth on a menu. Call it caldo plus or deluxe caldo, when caldo is described with meat, for it usually goes way beyond meat in a broth.

- *Caldo de pollo* (KAHL doh deh POH yoh). A brothy chicken soup, heavy on the chicken (perhaps a whole chicken thigh and leg), and with large chunks of vegetables, such as carrots, potatoes, and squash, plus garbanzos and corn, and perhaps a little rice thrown in. It's ordinarily served with tortillas or bolillos, lime wedges, chopped onions and chiles, or fresh salsa.

- *Caldo de pornil* (KAHL doh deh pohr NEEL). Pork broth and chunks of pork with many of the same ingredients as caldo de pollo.
- *Caldo de res* (KAHL doh deh rehs). Beef caldo is a meritorious brew featuring chunky pieces of beef, large chunks of potato, and enormous pieces of carrot.

Camarón (kah mah ROHN). Shrimp. The plural is *camarones* (kah mah ROH nehs).

Cambray (KAHM breh). A small onion or scallion.

Camote (kah MOH teh). Sweet potato. It's another gift from Mexico to the world.

Campo (KAHM poh). Something called *de campo* will mean farm fresh or from the countryside.

Canela (kah NEH lah). Cinnamon.

Cangrejos Moros (kahn GREH hohs MOH rohs). Stone crabs. (See also *Manitas de Cangrejo* and *Jaiba* below.)

Capeado (kah pee YAH doh). Fried vegetables with cheese, a Chiapas specialty. (See also Regional/Seasonal Specialties: *Capeado*.)

Capriotada (kah pree oh TAH dah). A more than wonderful bread pudding. It's made of thick slices of crusty bread drenched in piloncillo (brown sugar), and dribbled with chopped peanuts and raisins and perhaps a liqueur.

Capulínes (kah pooh LEE nehs). Black cherries.

Caracoles (kah rah KOH lehs). Snail or conch.

Carbón (kahr BOHN). Anything cooked over charcoal.

Carne (KAHR neh). Meat.

- *Carne adobado* (KAHR neh ah doh BAH doh). See *Adobo* above.
- *Carne asada* (KAHR neh ah SAH dah). This countrywide favorite is a thinly cut strip of broiled tenderloin or flank steak accompanied with grilled sweet pepper strips and onion slices. It's often paired with rice, refried beans, and guacamole.
- *Carne asada a la Tampiqueña* (KAHR neh ah SAH dah ah lah tahm pee KEH nyah). This well choreographed meal, with beef tenderloin as the centerpiece, is Mexico's supreme combination plate— the elaborate version of plain carne asada.

  In the thirties, José Loredo teamed broiled tenderloin with enchiladas, *rajas de chile poblano* (pepper strips grilled with onion and tomatoes), *frijoles* (beans); *chile relleno* (stuffed pepper), a taco, and guacamole. The platterful, dubbed *carne asada a la Tampiqueña*, became the rage at Loredo's Mexico City night spot, the Tampico Club. It's a staple on menus all over Mexico.

- *Carne de res* (KAHR neh deh rehs). Beef. Beef is also called *res* (rehs).
- *Carne de vaca* (KAHR neh deh BAH kah). Beef. Carne de res has the same meaning.
- *Carne guisada* (KAHR neh gwee SAH dah). A *norteño* (nohr TEH nyoh) or northern recipe created for beef that is flavorful, but rangy and tough. Browned lengths of steak are simmered in a *guiso* (stew) of onion, garlic, tomatoes, and chiles until the meat is tender.

Carnero (kahr DEH roh). Mutton. *Borrego* (boh REH goh) and *cordero* (kahr DEH roh) are other words for lamb.

Carnitas (kahr NEE tahs). Pork steamed and fried (in lard) that is served as a taco filling.

Casera (kah SEH rah). Homemade. The menu or a restaurant sign might advertise homemade food or *comida casera* (koh MEE dah kah SEH rah).

Catsup (KAHT soop). Ketchup.

Cazón (kah SOHN). Shark meat. It's used both dried and fresh. (See also Regional/Seasonal Specialties: *Cazón*.)

Cazuela (kah ZWEH lah). Casserole. The word is also used for the clay casserole container in which a dish may be prepared. *A la cazuela* (ah la kah ZWEH lah) would therefore appear on the menu.

Cebolla (SEH BOH yah). Onion.

- *Cebolla morada* (SEH BOH yah moh RAH dah). Red or purple onion.
- *Cebollas a la parrillada* (SEH BOH yahs ah lah pah ree YAH dah). Grilled green onions, also called *rajas* (RAH hahs).
- *Cebollos de Rabo* (SEH BOH yahs deh RAH boh). The phrase for scallions.

Cecina (SEH SEE nah). A thin cut of salted pork or beef that's marinated and then grilled. (See also *Tasajo* below and Regional/Seasonal Specialties: *Cecina*.)

Cemitas (seh MEE tahs). A sandwich served in the states of Puebla and Tlaxcala. (See Regional/Seasonal Specialties: *Cemitas*.)

Cerdo (SEHR doh). Pork. Another word for pork is *puerco* (pooh EHR koh).

Cereza (seh REH sah). Cherry.

Ceviche (seh BEE cheh). Uncooked seafood marinated in fresh lime juice. The name is thought to have evolved from *cebar* (seh BAHR) (to saturate), while the dish is believed to have originated in Peru, by way of the Polynesian Islands. Bite-size-to-smaller chopped pieces of raw fish, shrimp, lobster, scallops, octopus, or whatever seafood is fresh, are marinated in lime juice for several hours, then tossed with chiles, tomatoes, onion, cilantro, and sometimes olive oil. It may be served on a plate with crisp tortillas or in a goblet with crackers or chips. (For local variations see Regional/Seasonal Specialties: *Ceviche.*)

Chalupa (cha LOO pah). A canoe-shaped botana. The word comes from the shape of small boats used by the Aztecs on the canals of Tenochtitlán, which the thick tortilla cakes, used as the base for chalupas, are sometimes shaped like, with the edges pinched to hold the filling. These tasty treats are usually topped with a thin layer of tomato or adobo sauce, over which is sprinkled a bit of ground meat or crumbled cooked sausage and finished off with crumbled cheese, fresh onions, and sometimes a sprinkling of chopped lettuce. In some places similar morsels are also known as *gorditas* (gohr DEE tahs) or *tlacoyos* (tlah KOH yohs). Crisp, open-faced Tex Mex–style fried corn tortillas called chalupas in the United States are known as *tostadas* (tohs TAH dahs) in Mexico. (See also *gorditas, tlacoyos tostada* below, and Regional/Seasonal Specialties: *Chalupa.*)

Champiñón (cham peen YOHN). Mushroom. *Hongo* and *seta* are other words for mushroom.

Chanclas (CHAN klahs). A sauce-covered sandwich that's a specialty of Puebla. (See also Regional/Seasonal Specialties: *Chanclas*.)

Changleta (chan GLEH tah). A dessert of sweet stuffed chayote that's a specialty of Chiapas. (See also *Chayote* below and Regional/Seasonal Specialties: *Changleta*.)

Chapulines (cha poo LEE nehs). Dried grasshoppers. Though more of a specialty in Oaxaca than elsewhere, protein-rich dried grasshoppers also turn up in restaurants serving pre-Hispanic specialties. When served or offered by restaurants or street vendors, they are usually meant to be a munchie with alcoholic drinks—sort of a substitute for peanuts or popcorn.

Charales (chah RAH lehs). A small dried silvery fish similar to a minnow. Around Lake Pátzcuaro and Lake Chapala, where they are harvested, they are sold by the bagful for munching with beer, or for use in tacos. (See also *Topotes* below and Regional/Seasonal Specialties: *Charales*.)

Chaya (CHA yah). A spinach-like, vitamin-rich, large green leaf with a taste that's similar to spinach but with the consistency of kale when boiled. It's used in eggs the way spinach might be mixed in. It's also mixed with masa for several Maya tamales. This versatile leaf also blends into a smooth health drink that's sweetened with honey or sugar.

Chayote (cha YOH teh). A spiny green squash called merliton or vegetable pear in the United States, it has several varieties in Mexico. A native plant, usually diced or sliced and boiled, it finds its way into soups and salads, and is served as a dessert, and as a garnish for meat. (See also *Changleta* above.)

Chia (CHEE ah). A seed used to make a drink. (See also Beverages A to Z: *Aguas Frescas.*)

Chícaros (CHEE cha rohs). Peas.

Chicharrón (chee cha ROHN). Fried pork rind. Street vendors sell it in huge, torso-sized pieces that have been deep-fried. Patrons select flavorings to add on top such as a dribble of mild red chile sauce or a sprinkling of chile powder and fresh lime. In some places momocho is the word for chicharrón. (See also Regional/Seasonal Specialties: *Monguls* and *Salsa de Chicharrón.*)

Chilacayote (chee lah kah YOH teh). A bright green, round squash that's also transformed into a candied dessert.

Chilaquiles (chee lah KEE lehs). A casserole that's a popular, robust breakfast choice. It's sometimes made with scrambled eggs and chorizo (sausage), but always with day-old tortillas cut in strips or wedges, white onion, melted cheese, sour cream, green chiles, and is sprinkled with crumbled cheese.

It can be primarily green if made with a green sauce, or red if a red sauce is the cook's choice. It's a staple of breakfast buffets although it's also served for lunch with chicken substituting for the eggs.

Chile Atole (CHEE leh ah TOH leh). Not to be confused with sweet atole (see *Atole* above), this is more like a soup, with a base ingredient of finely ground cooked corn masa, visible pieces of corn, and green chiles to give it a bite. It's served warm in a glass or a cup.

Chile Relleno (CHEE leh reh YEH noh). A large tangy poblano pepper usually stuffed with chewy white cheese, beans, or picadillo, but occasionally with shrimp or beans, then dipped in batter and fried until the pepper is firm/soft but not mushy. If it's picante it will be only mildly so.

Chiles (CHEE lehs). Chiles. Once the conquerors of Mexico introduced to Spain the chiles they discovered in Mexico, chiles were swallowed into many of the world's cuisines. In Mexican markets they're heaped in a staggering number of fresh and dried versions. (See below.) Many are also bottled and sold in every grocery store in Mexico. Bowls of chiles, marinated in vinegar, are combined with onions and carrots and other vegetables as a table condiment called *encurtidos* (ehn koor TEE dohs). (See also Market Buying Tips: *Chiles*.)

Chiles Fresco (CHEE lehs FREHS koh). Fresh (as opposed to dried) chiles.

- *Chilaca* (chee LAH kah). These mild peppers are a darker green than a jalapeño and two-thirds the girth. Its dried form, the *pasilla* (pah SEE yah), is used in many sauces.
- *Güero* (GWEH roh). Yellow-green, hot, and long (hand-length), the güero looks like a banana pepper, which is one of its other names. It's also known as Hungarian pepper.
- *Habanero* (ah bah NEH roh). Though small (about golf-ball size) and rumple-skinned (like a mandarin orange)—it's considered to be the hottest pepper of all. Luckily it's found mostly in bottles and not cooked in the food. But bottled habaneros are sometimes placed on restaurant tables, so venture into them slowly.
- *Jalapeño* (hah lah PEH nyoh). Finger-length and meaty, these provide the heat in some salsas and other dishes. When allowed to fully ripen they are red. When the red form is dried it's called called *chipotle* (chee POHT leh).
- *Manzano* (mahn ZAH noh). This pale orange pepper is shaped like a tomato, though much smaller, and is the fresh version of the dried *cascabel* (kahs kah behl).
- *Poblano* (poh BLAH noh). Vaguely arrow-shaped and mildly hot, the poblano is either green or red (when ripe). When dried the red poblano is called

ancho (AHN cho) or *mulato* (moo lah toh). The poblano is used for stuffed pepper, called *chile relleno* (CHEE leh reh YEH noh), described above. It's about the length and girth of a small female hand and usually carries a little heat.

- *Serrano* (seh RRAH noh). The slender, green serrano is deceptively heat-packed for its size, which is the girth of a pencil, and about a joint less than an index finger in length. It's used in *moles* (MOH lehs), and in both red and green salsas. Small mounds of chopped serranos, along with chopped white onion and cilantro, are served to accompany soup and tacos—go easy on the fiery serranos. (See also *Chiles Secos* [dried chiles] below.)

Chiles Nogada (CHEE lehs en noh GAH dah). A sweetish meat-stuffed poblano pepper served around Independence Day. (See also Regional/Seasonal Specialties: *Chiles en nogada*.)

Chiles Secos (CHEE lehs SEH kohs). Dried chiles.

- *Amarillo* (ah mah REE yoh). Yellow and slender, in a size similar to a serrano, the amarillo is plenty fiery. It's used in yellow mole. Amarillo chiles are also called *chilcosle* (cheel KOHS leh).
- *Ancho* (AHN choh). The reddish-black ancho, a dried poblano, is hotter in its dried state. The ancho looks very much like a mulato chile.

- *Árbol* (AHR bohl). A long thin, very hot, pepper.
- *Cascabel* (kahs kah BEHL). The hot cascabel is a dried manzano. It is almost acorn-like in shape and size.
- *Chipotle* (chee POHT leh). The dried version of the *jalapeño* (hah lah PAY nyoh) after it's ripened to red. The heat factor increases in the dried form and use of it has been known to force some unwary tourists to beg for mercy and the fire hose.
- *Guajillo* (gwah HEE yoh). A mild, long but plump pepper used in many sauces.
- *Morita* (moh REE tah). Comes in small and large sizes both of which will fuel the furnace.
- *Mulato* (moo LAH toh). The mildly hot mulato is slightly larger than an ancho chile, but looks much like it; both are dried forms of the poblano. The ancho is frequently substituted for the mulato.
- *Pasilla* (pah SEE yah). As long as an index finger and about a finger-and-a-half wide, this red chile is used in many cooking sauces.
- *Piquín* (pee KEEN). A tiny and extremely hot chile.

Chilmole (cheel MOH leh). A savory black chile paste used primarily in Yucatecan sauces. It's also called *chirmole* (cheer MOH leh), *relleno negro* (reh YEH noh NEH groh) and *recado negro* (reh KAH doh NEH groh). It's served over turkey and used to flavor black beans. (See also Regional/Seasonal Specialties: *Chilmole* and *Pavo* and Market Buying Tips: *Chilmole*.)

Chilorio (chee loh REE oh). Shredded pork cooked in a sauce of chiles, garlic, cumin, oregano, and other spices mixed with vinegar.

Chilpachole (cheel pah CHO leh). A chile sauce used for stews that's a specialty of Veracruz. (See also Regional/Seasonal Specialties: *Chilpachole.*)

Chimichanga (chee mee CHAN gah). A large tortilla that's stuffed and deep-fried. (See also *Burrito* above.)

Chirmole (cheer MOH leh). A blackened chile sauce. (See also *Chilmole* above and Regional/Seasonal Specialties: *Chilmole.*)

Chocolate (cho koh LAH teh). Chocolate. The Aztec emperor Moctezuma drank this beverage just before setting off for a conjugal visit, which intrigued the Spanish conquerors, who introduced it to the rest of the world via Spain. Possibly its alleged aphrodisiac qualities were an incentive for the Spaniards to mix it more palatably with sugar instead of ground chiles, which Moctezuma favored. Cortés, however, mentioned only its stimulating/invigorating qualities when he reported on it to King Charles V of Spain. Called "drink of the gods" chocolate or *cacao* (kah KAH oh), the beans were also used as money by the Aztecs. Where it was grown, the beans were given as forced tribute by the populace to the Aztec emperor. Presumably he had so many of the beans he could afford the decadent consumption of them in a drink.

(See also *Chocolate* entries in Regional/Seasonal Specialties and Market Buying Tips.)

Chongos Zamoranos (CHON gohs sah moh RAH nohs). A sweet milk and cinnamon dessert. Milk, sugar, cinnamon, and egg yolks are curdled then cooked until a thickened dessert is created. It's a very popular dessert among Mexicans.

Chorizo (cho REE soh). A fatty, deep red, pork sausage. Flavor-enhancing aromatic spices and chiles also provide its characteristic color. It's fried and mixed with eggs at breakfast and used as a taco filling often paired with potatoes.

Chuleta de cerdo (chooh LEH tah deh SEHR doh). Pork chop.

Churro (CHOO rroh). A tube-shaped, deep-fried fritter. A gift from Spain, this six- to eight-inch long (or longer) fritter is rolled in sugar while it's hot. The irresistible deluxe version comes with its hollow tube-like center filled with chocolate or cajeta, or the outside is given a stream of condensed milk. Churros are found at almost all festivals and sold in the evenings on street corners. A few restaurants, called *churrerías* (choo rreh REE ahs) specialize in churros served with traditional hot chocolate and atole.

Cilantro (see LAHN troh). Fresh coriander also known as Chinese parsley. This flat, green leafy herb, sold in bunches in American and Mexican groceries and outdoor markets, is responsible for the pungent flavor—between sage and lemon peel—that is the heart and soul of many Mexican dishes.

Ciruela (seer ooh REH lah). Prune.

Claro de Huevo (KLAH roh deh WEH boh). Egg whites.

Clavos (KLAH bohs). Cloves.

Clemole (cleh MOH leh). A stewlike specialty found in Taxco, Guerrero. (See also Regional/Seasonal Specialties: *Clemole*.)

Cocer al Vapor (koh SEHR ahl bah POHR). Steam-cooked.

Cochinita (koh chee NEE tah). Suckling pig. *Cochinita pibil* (koh chee NEE tah pee BEEL) is Yucatecán-style pig baked in a ground pit called a *pib* (peeb). It's steam-baked in a banana-leaf wrapper holding the meat in a marinade made with the flavorful mild achiote preparado, and tomatoes and onions. Though once relegated to Yucatecan menus only, this has crossed state borders to appear on menus outside the Yucatán. *Lechón* is another word for suckling pig.

Cocina (koh CEE nah). Kitchen.

Coco (KOH koh). Coconut.

Coco Fresco (KOH koh FREHS koh). Fresh coconut milk. Sellers of this treat whack off the top of the coconut, pop a straw in the hole, and serve the beverage in its original container. Often the coconuts are chilled so the drink is especially refreshing. (See also Beverages A to Z: *Coco Fresco.*)

Col (kohl). Cabbage. Cabbage is often substituted for lettuce.

Coliflor (koh lee FLOHR). Cauliflower.

Coloradito (koh loh rah DEE toh). A darkish, lightly fruity tasting mole. It's made with chiles, sesame seeds, almonds, raisins, bananas, and other fruits, and a variety of spices into a sauce that's ladled over chicken. (See also *Mole* below, Regional/Seasonal Specialties: *Mole,* and Market Buying Tips: *Mole* and *Pipián.*)

Combinado (kohm bee NAH doh). This literally means combined, but the word usually describes a combination plate or *plato combinado* (PLAH toh kohm beeh NAH doh) or a sampler platter.

Comida (koh MEE dah). Food or lunch. A restaurant sign or a notice on the menu might read *comida del día* (koh MEE dah del DEE ah) or *comida corrida* (koh MEE dah koh REE dah), which means lunch meal of the day.

Comida Casera (koh MEE dah kah SEH rah). Home-made food. A sign on a restaurant or menu might indicate that the food is comida casera, or the waiter might say *tipo casera* (TEE poh kah SAY rah), meaning homemade-type food is served.

Comino (koh MEE noh). Cumin.

Conejo (koh NEH hoh). Rabbit. (See also *Mixiotes* below.)

Consomé (kohn soh MEH). Consommé. A light chicken broth soup usually containing rice, shredded chicken, and sprinkled with a few pieces of white onion.

Corazón (koh rah SOHN). Heart.

Cordero (kohr DEH roh). Lamb. (See also *Borrego* and *Carnero* above.)

Cordoniz (kohr doh NEEZ). Quail.

Corunda (koh ROON dah). A triangular-shaped Michoacán-style tamal. (See also Regional/Seasonal Specialties: *Tamales*.)

Cosida a la Madrilena (koh SEE dah ah lah mah dree LEH nah). A clear brothy soup made with bacon, pork, and large white asturias beans.

Costilla (kohs TEE yah). Rib.

Crema (KREH mah). Cream. Mexican crema used to ladle on cecina (salted pork or beef) or on strawberries is rich, thick as pudding, and lightly sweet—a true cultural treat. A sandwich or hot dog may be offered with a choice of this Mexican crema, along with *salsa cruda*. The combination is refreshingly tasty. Coffee cream is *crema para café* (KREH mah PAH rah kah FEH).

Crema Agria (KREH mah AH gree yah). Sour cream. U.S.-style sour cream is seldom served in Mexico. The substitute is thick and rich Mexican crema, which, while not the same thing, makes an interesting change from sour cream. (See also *Crema* above.)

Crema de Cacahuate (KREH mah deh kah kah WAH teh). Peanut butter. It may also be called *Mantequilla de Cacahuate*.

Crepas (KREH pahs). Crepes.

Criadillas (cree ah DEE yahs). Bull testicles. What's jokingly labeled "mountain oysters" in the United States is considered a delicacy that is served either fried or in a sauce in Mexico.

Croquetas (kroh KEH tahs). Croquettes.

Crudo (KROO doh). Raw.

Cuitlacoche (kweet lah KOH cheh). A black fungus that grows on corn. (See also *Huitlacoche* below.)

Datil (dah TEEL). Date.

Deshebrado (deh seh BRAH doh). Shredded. Meats are often shredded for use in stews, soups, and salads.

Dona (DOH nah). Doughnut.

Dorado (doh RAH doh). Mahimahi fish.

Dulce/Dulces (DOOL seh/DOOL sehs). Sweets. Something sweet is dulce. Dulces can mean candy, cookies, or the candied fruits that abound in Mexico. Yams, figs, limes, oranges, tamarinds, coconuts, brown sugar, and milk all wind up on the sweet shop shelf in tantalizing shapes and sizes demonstrating Mexico's serious sweet tooth. (See also Regional/Seasonal Specialties: *Dulces* and Market Buying Tips: *Dulce.*)

Durazno (dooh RAHZ noh). Peach.

Ejotes (eh HOH tehs). String beans.

Elote (eh LOH teh). Large-kernel corn on the cob. Tubs of fresh steaming corn on the cob appear nightly, and even in the daytime, on streets all over

Mexico as a kind of fast-food snack. Choose a slathering of mayonnaise for flavor or a sprinkle of mild chile powder—or both. Miniature corn is called *elotito* (ay loh TEE toh).

Empanada (em pah NAH dah). A meat turnover. Spicy ground meat fills a clam-shaped flour dough wrapper that is baked or fried.

Empanizada (em pah nee SAH dah). Breaded. Mexicans fry a lot of food, but bread very little of it.

En Adobo (en ah DOH boh). See *Adobo* above.

Encarcelada (en kar seh LAH dah). Shelled.

Encebollada (en seh boh YAH dah). Cooked in onions.

Enchilada (en chee LAH dah). An enchilada is a tortilla that has been given a quick bath in hot oil, a dip into a chile sauce, and rolled up around cheese, or meat, then ladled with a green or red chile sauce, and baked. (Besides those listed below, see also Regional/Seasonal Specialties: *Enchiladas*.)

- *Enchiladas adobados* (en chee LAH dahs ah doh BAH dohs). Beef or chicken enchiladas in a sauce of ground chiles, herbs, spices, and vinegar. (See also *Adobo* above.)
- *Enchiladas rojas* (en chee LAH dahs ROH hahs).

Meat- or cheese-filled enchiladas with a red chile ancho sauce. These are the most common enchiladas on menus.

- *Enchiladas suisas* (en chee LAH dahs SWEE sahs). Swiss-style enchiladas. This mild and rich enchilada rendition is chicken- or cheese-filled enchiladas in a mild cream-tomato sauce flavored with a hint of nutmeg.
- *Enchiladas verdes* (en chee LAH dahs BEHR dehs). Topped with a piquant but delicate green tomatillo sauce.

Encurtidos (en koohr TEE dohs). Fresh-cut vegetables and chiles in vinegar. Placed on the table as an accompaniment to the meal, they look tasty and they are—but they're not always as innocent as they appear. These tempting-looking bowls may either contain something deadly hot or morsels that are quite mild and delicious when dabbled on top of bread or crackers or eaten with a meat dish.

Eneldo (eh NEHL doh). Dill.

Enfriolada (en free oh LAH dah). Anything in a bean sauce. The word is usually used to announce corn tortillas bathed in a smooth black bean sauce and topped with thinly sliced white onions and crumbled cheese. Other toppings which might appear include hard-boiled eggs, shredded chicken breast, and pieces of tasajo or cecina.

Enmolada (en moh LAH dah). Anything bathed in a mole sauce.

En Nogada (en oh GAH dah). In an almond sauce or with almonds.

En Papillote (en pah pee YOH teh). Meat or fish baked in a paper or foil wrapper. Traditionally the paper is a thin one made from maguey fibers, but tinfoil is a common substitute.

Ensalada (en sah LAH dah). Salad. Salad that comes with a plate lunch may be no more than a few pieces of lettuce or cabbage topped with a bit of tomato and onion. But it can be much more if ordered separately or selected from a U.S.-style salad bar. Better restaurants, and those catering to many tourists, can assure that the fresh vegetables used are purified and safe for eating. Another popular salad, which has no name, often accompanies sandwiches. It's a combination of boiled and diced potatoes and carrots with green peas mixed together with mayonnaise. (Besides those listed below, see also *Aderezo* above for dressings and Regional/Seasonal Specialties: *Ensalada de Noche Buena*.)

• *Ensalada César* (en sah LAH dah SEH sahr). Caesar salad. From its Tijuana birthplace it leapfrogged to far distant lands and can be found on menus in all of Mexico's better restaurants. It, of course, comes with its own special dressing made with raw egg yolks, olive oil, vinegar, wine, mustard, salt, Worcestershire sauce, and grated Parmesan cheese. César Cardini, an Italian immigrant and owner of Hotel César in Tijuana, created this salad in his hotel restaurant in 1925. Anchovies are frequently featured in this salad but the original ensalada cesár didn't have them. As delicious as the dressing is, be aware that raw egg yolks can be dangerous, even deadly.

- *Ensalada mixta* (en sah LAH dah MEEKS tah). Salad in Mexico can be a wonderful mix of crisp lettuce, brilliant red tomatoes, cucumber, peas, avocado, and rings of fresh onions. The occasional salad bar in Mexico may offer a selection similar to those in the United States.

- *Ensalada de vegetales* (en sah LAH dah deh beh hee TAH lehs). Vegetable salad. This may be a salad of cooked vegetables, a mix of fresh greens, or a combination of the two.

En Su Propio Jugo (en soo PRO pee oh HOO goh). In its own juice. Menus will use this phrase to refer to how a meat or seafood is prepared.

Entomatado (en toh mah TAH doh). Literally, this means in a tomato sauce. As a dish this usually means corn tortillas covered with a mild tomato sauce, sprinkled with crumbled cheese and sliced white onions.

Epazote (eh pah SOH teh). A pungent herb known by the unappealing name of wormseed, it's used frequently in quesadillas, frijoles, and sauces. Totally unlike any other herb, it's somewhat medicinal, woody, and minty in aroma and taste. In beans it's said to reduce the flatulent effect. (See also Market Buying Tips: *Epazote*.)

Escabeche (ehs kah BEH cheh). Pickled.

Escalopas (ehs KA loh pahs). Scallops.

Escamole (ehs kah MOH leh). Ant eggs. This true delicacy of pre-Hispanic Mexican cuisine looks like rice and tastes wonderful especially if sautéed in wine and butter. The dish may accompany meat or be ordered alone and served with tortillas, chopped onions, lettuce, and avocado.

Escocesa (ehs koh SEH sah). A vegetable soup.

Espageti (ehs pah GHEH tee). Spaghetti. (See also *Spaghetti* below.)

Espárragos (ehs PAH rrah gohs). Asparagus.

Especias (ehs PEH see yahs). Spices. The waiter may be able to tell you what spices are used to prepare a dish. (See also Market-Buying Tips: *Especias*.)

Espinaca (ehs pee NAH kah). Spinach.

Esquites (ehs KEE tehs). Fried sweet corn.

Estación (ehs tah see OHN). Season. On a menu, *estación* is primarily used to say something is offered if it's in season.

Estilo (ehs TEE loh). Style. The menu may say that something is in the style of a particular well-known food or is a food prepared in the style of a place, such as Puebla *(poblano)*, Veracruz *(veracruzana)*, the north *(el Norte)*, Guadalajara *(tapatío)*, etc. The same idea is also expressed if something is *a la* (ah lah) a particular place, such as a la Veracruz, meaning the dish is served the way it's prepared in Veracruz.

Estofado (ehs toh FAH doh). An amber-colored mole. It's refreshingly tasty, with a unique flavor and color derived from finely ground tomatoes, almonds, bread, raisins, cloves, and ground guajillo chiles. Depending on the cook's proportions of sweet ingredients to spicy ones, the dish may be lightly spicy hot or sweet and spicy. It's served over chicken.

Ezquites (ehz KEE tehs). A corn medley. Fresh corn cooked with butter, epazote, and onions is given a tangy flair with table-added condiments of fresh lime juice, chile powder, and grated white cheese.

Faisán (fah ee SAHN). Pheasant.

Fajitas (fah HEE tahs). Strips of grilled skirt steak. In the United States this meat dish is served with tortillas, guacamole, rice, and beans. It has a close cousin in Mexico, but it can be a disappointing choice since the same marinades and grilling techniques used in the United States aren't employed.

Fiambre (fee YAHM breh). Cold meat.

Fideo (fee DEH oh). Vermicelli.

Filete (fee LEH teh). Fillet of fish, shrimp, beef, or pork.

Fina (FEE nah). Fine. A menu might describe a salad with fine herbs or *hierbas finas* (YEHR bahs FEE nahs).

Flameado (flah meh YAH doh). Flamed. A flameado dish will usually be prepared as a dramatic, flaming tableside event.

Flan (flahn). A caramel egg custard flavored with vanilla. There are several variations of this wonderful dessert so you're never sure which one will arrive to tantalize your tastebuds. Flan Napoletan (nah poh leh TAHN) is white and thicker than the custard-style flan, and may be flavored with liqueur.

Flautas (FLOUT ahs). A stuffed, deep-fried, tube-shaped tortilla. Corn tortillas filled in the middle with a small helping of chicken, pork, or beef, are then tightly rolled "flute-shaped," fried to a golden, crunchy brown, and served hot with sour cream and sometimes sliced tomatoes, onions, and crumbled cheese. This same dish is also known as *tacos dorados* (TAH kohs doh RAH dohs); without the garnish it's a *taquito* (tah KEE toh).

Flor/Flores (flohr/FLOH rehs). Flower/flowers. Pre-Hispanic cooking favored many flowers, among them those of the maguey, sotol, squash, and bean. These are considered gourmet food now and find their way into soups, quesadillas, and crepes to name just a few dishes.

Flor de Calabaza (flohr deh cah lah BAH sah). Large orange delicate squash blossoms used in soup and crepes.

Frambuesa (frahm BWEH sah). Raspberry.

Fresa (FREH sah). Strawberry. *Fresas con crema* (FREH sahs kohn KREH mah) means strawberries and cream. Celaya and Irapuato, in central Mexico, provide strawberries for the country.

Fresco (FREHS koh). Fresh.

Freír/Frito (freh EER/FREE toh). To fry/fried. Fried foods were introduced by the Spaniards. Indian communities in Mexico, even today, boil, broil, and bake food instead of frying it.

Fría/Frío (FREE ah/FREE oh). Cold. The menu might announce *carnes frías* (KAHR nehs FREE ahs) meaning cold meats or *bebidas frías* (beh BEE dehs FREE ahs) meaning cold drinks.

Frijoles (free HOH lehs). Beans. Nearly 100 varieties of beans are included in Mexico's cuisine, although the pinto is probably the best known. Frijoles were another of Mexico's gifts to the world.

- *Frijoles borracho* (free HOH lehs boh RRAH choh). Drunk is the translation of borracho, so these are "drunken beans" made just like the cowgirl's beans below with the addition of stale beer—delicious.
- *Frijoles a la charra* (free HOH lehs ah lah CHAH rrah). Cowgirl's beans. These beans are, literally, by the hand of a lady charro, meaning with pork rind, fried tomatoes, onion, and cilantro and served as a soup.
- *Frijoles negros* (free HOH lehs NEH grohs). Black beans. Traditionally, black beans are served on the Gulf Coast primarily in the state of Veracruz, and on the Pacific Coast south of Acapulco. They're seasoned with a sprig of epazote, and served mashed and refried or as a whole-bean or pureed soup and may be crowned with white cheese and chopped onions.
- *Frijoles refritos* (free HOH lehs reh FREE tohs). The ubiquitous dollop of mashed pinto beans served with most Mexican meals is not refried

beans, as is commonly thought, but well-fried beans. Lard provides some of the flavor in this pastelike recipe.

Fritada (free TAH dah). *Cabrito* (kid) fried in its own blood. (See also *Cabrito* above.)

Fruta (FROO tah). Fruit. Mexico abounds in common and exotic fresh tropical fruit.

Galleta (gah YEH tah). Cookie or cracker.

Gallina (gah YEE nah). Hen.

Gambas (GAHM bahs). Large shrimp.

Ganso (GAHN soh). Goose.

Garnacha (gahr NAH cha). A Yucatecan botana. (See also Regional/Seasonal Specialties: *Botana*.)

Genebre (heh NEH breh). Ginger.

Gordita (gohr DEE tah). Describing a gordita precisely can be as difficult as describing Mexico's chiles; a gordita in one part of Mexico bears no resemblance to a gordita in another part. It can be a sweet cookie or more often a savory botana. Even as a botana it has many widely different regional variations. Sometimes it's large enough to make a meal. Though gordita ordering is always a culinary adventure, it's ordinarily not disappointing. (See also *Chalupa* above and Regional/Seasonal Specialties: *Botana.*)

Granada (grah NAH dah). Pomegranate. The shiny red seeds of the pomegranate complete the presentation of chiles en nogada, which are served in August and September when the fruit is in season.

Grano (GRAH noh). Grain.

Granola (grah NO lah). Granola. It's easy to find on breakfast menus and breakfast buffets along with yogurt, honey, and fresh fruit. But packaged granola is rare.

Guacamole (gwah kah MOH leh). Mashed avocado flavored with freshly chopped tomato, cilantro, and garlic. It accompanies tacos, steak, and Mexican specialties. It's also served as an appetizer with tortilla chips.

Guajolote (gwah hoh LOH teh). Turkey. (See also *pavo* below.)

Guanábana (wah NAH bah nah). A tropical fruit. Dotted with thornless black-tipped humps on the outside, the dark green outer layer covers a fragrant yellow pulp. It's used in *aguas frescas,* and as a dessert. (See also Beverages A to Z: *Aguas Frescas.*)

Guarnación (gwahr nah see OHN). Garnish.

Guinatán (gwee nah TAHN). Salted fish.

Guiso/Guisado (GWEE soh/gwee SAH doh). Stew/stewed.

Gusanos de Maguey (goo SAH nohs deh MAH geh). A worm that lives in maguey, that's collected and served fried. It's the same worm that's seen in bottles of mezcal, a distilled liquor. (See also Beverages A to Z: *Mezcal*.)

Haba (AH bah). A large bean used in soup and stew.

Helado (eh LAH doh). Ice cream. Good restaurants usually have refrigeration capable of keeping ice cream sufficiently cold. Ice cream shops, however, often sell ice cream that's soft and mushy, and thus not properly refrigerated. It could cause a health problem.

Hervida (ehr BEEH dah). Boiled.

Hielo (YEH loh). Ice. In Mexico it's important to be sure that ice is made from purified water. Ask, *¿Es purificado el hielo?* (ehs poo ree fee KAH doh el YEH loh) to see if the ice is purified. Restaurants catering to a significant number of tourists use only safe ice. If in doubt, order drinks *sin hielo* (seen YEH loh), which means without ice. *Con hielo* (kohn YEH loh) means with ice.

Generally speaking, ice that has been chipped or

shaved from a block is almost uniformly *not* made with purified water. Ice cubes formed into a cylinder and with a hole through the middle *probably* came from an ice plant using purified water. Some people avoid ice completely, just to be safe.

Hierba (YEHR bah). Herb.

Hierba Buena (YEHR bah BWEH nah). Mint. It's also spelled *yerba buena*.

Hierba Santa (YEHR bah SAHN tah). A large, soft, anise-flavored leaf used in sauces and for flavoring. It's also called Hoja Santa (OH hah SAHN tah).

Higado (ee GAH doh). Liver.

Higado Encebollado (ee GAH doh en SEH boh YAH doh). Liver and onions.

Higo (EE goh). Fig.

Hinojo (ee NOH hoh). Fennel.

Hojas (OH hahs). Leaves. Mexican cooks use many leaves in cooking including that of the banana or *plátano* (PLAH tah noh), *maguey* (MAH geh), corn or *maíz* (mah EEZ), and avocado or *aguacate* (ah wah KAH teh). Banana, corn stalk leaves, and corn husks called *hojas secas de maíz* (OH hahs SEH kahs deh mah EEZ) are all used to wrap tamales for steaming. Avocado leaves give flavor to cooked sauces. *Hoja Santa* (OH hah SAHN tah) is a large, anise-flavored leaf. A thin membrane of maguey leaf holds *mixiotes* (mee SHOH tehs), which is meat wrapped in parchment paper and steamed in a rich broth. Leaves of the maguey and banana, besides acting as aromatic wrappers for food, are used to line earthen cooking pits or cover the food that's cooked in them. Cooks are faithful in their use of leaves because of the subtle flavor imparted by them.

Hongo (OHN goh). Mushroom. *Champiñón* and *seta* are other words for mushroom.

Horneado (ohr neh AH doh). Baked.

Horno (OHR noh). Oven. Something al horno will be oven-baked.

Horno de Lena (OHR noh deh LEH nah). Wood-fired oven.

Huachinango (wah chee NAHN goh). Red snapper. Huauchinango a la Veracruzana hails from the port city of Veracruz where red snapper is smothered in a tomato sauce (with a hint of cloves and cinnamon), garlic, onions, jalapeño peppers, and green olives. Though it originated in Veracruz, it's a staple on seafood menus countrywide.

Hualumbos (wah LOOM bohs). Fried maguey flowers. The flowers are dipped in a delicious light batter and fried.

Huauzontle (wah ZOHNT leh). A leafy, slightly broccoli-flavored plant. It's among the pre-Hispanic specialties handed down from the Aztecs. The tender, upper part of the plant is boiled and then dipped in an egg batter and fried.

Huevos (WEH bohs). Eggs.

- *Huevos charros* (WEH bohs CHAH rohs). A close cousin to huevos rancheros are huevos charros, featuring eggs and chicharrón (pork rind) on a tortilla in either a green or red sauce.
- *Huevos Divorceados* (WEH bohs dee bohr seh AH dohs). Divorced eggs. This is a catchy name for two fried eggs, one covered in green sauce and the other in a red sauce.
- *Huevos con Machaca* (WEH bohs kohn mah CHAH kah). Eggs are mixed with machaca, which is beef that's been dried, salted, and shredded. Though a northern Mexico specialty, this favorite among Mexicans leaped state lines for placement on menus much farther south. It's served with a red sauce and tortillas.
- *Huevos a la Méxicana* (WEH bohs ah lah MEH hee kah nah). Eggs scrambled with onions, tomatoes, and chiles.
- *Huevos Motuleños*. (WEH bohs moh tooh LEHN

yohs). This hearty platterful displays a fried egg atop a fried tortilla covered with ham, peas, onions, and a tomato sauce. Though it originated in the town of Motul, Yucatán, it's on menus all over the country.

- *Huevos de Naca* (WEH bohs deh NAH kah). Fish roe.
- *Huevos Rancheros* (WEH bohs rahn CHEH rohs). Ranch-style eggs. A lightly fried tortilla is spread with a bean sauce, topped with a fried egg, and drenched with a tomato sauce. The name may sound countryfied but this breakfast special is prepared in every restaurant with a breakfast menu.
- *Huevos Refritos* (WEH bohs reh FREE tohs). Fried eggs.
- *Huevos Revueltos* (WEH bohs reh booh EHL tohs). Scrambled eggs.
- *Huevos Tibios* (WEH bohs TEE bee ohs). Soft-boiled eggs.
- *Huevos a la Veracruzana* (WEH bohs ah lah beh rah kroo SAH nah). Eggs Veracruz-style are wrapped in a corn tortilla smothered in beans and topped with cheese and green chiles. (See also Comfort Foods: Eggs and Market Buying Tips: *Huevos*.)

Huitlacoche (weeht lah KOH cheh). Corn fungus. Also spelled *cuitlacoche*, this Mexican delicacy is a black fungus found growing on corn during the rainy season. The delicious huitlacoche flavor is slightly that of mushrooms with an overtone of corn. Featured in crepes, scrambled eggs, and soups, this pre-Hispanic food has risen to the status of alta cocina Méxicana.

Itacates (eeh tah KAH tehs). Hidalgo-style corn gorditas eaten as a botana or full meal. Itacates also refers to leftovers a hostess might pack up for guests to take home. (See also Regional/Seasonal Specialties: *Botana*.)

Jaiba (HI bah). Crab. The word usually refers to the edible blue crab found in Gulf Coast waters off Campeche, which is part of Mexico's Yucatán Peninsula. Stone crabs are called *cangrejos moros* (kahn GREH hohs MOH rohs). (See also *Manitas de Cangrejo* below.)

Jalapeño (hah lah PEH nyoh). A hot green chile. (See also *Chiles Fresco* above.)

Jamón (hah MOHN). Ham.

Jarra/Jarro (HAH rrah/HAH rroh). A jarra is a large clay pitcher, but a glass pitcher may also be called a jarra. A jarro is a small pitcher or a small cup shaped like a pitcher.

Jícama (HEE kah mah). A large crunchy turnip/potato–looking tuber that is faintly sweet and tastes like a cross between celery, potato, water chestnut, and coconut. Street vendors sell it sliced fresh and garnished with red chile powder and fresh lime.

Jitomate (hee toh MAH teh). Tomato. Also called *tomate rojo* (toh MAH tay ROH hoh). Mexico's gift to the world became so when the Spanish conquerors returned to Spain with this unique fruit. Mexican cooks favor the small Roma tomato in cooking although any tomato will do.

Jugo (HOOH goh). Juice. Juice bars, featuring fresh fruit drinks, are popular in Mexico, with the juice prepared while you wait. Excellent canned fruit drinks are also available. (See also Market Buying Tips: *Jugo* and Beverages A to Z: *Aguas Frescas* and *Liquada*.)

Lagrima de Obispo (LAH gree mah deh oh BEES poh). Literally "tears of the bishop." This Puebla dish is sweet camote (pumpkin), chirmoya (an exotic fruit), and pineapple scattered with pine nuts and sugar pearls.

Langosta (lahn GOHS tah). Lobster. Fresh lobster is abundant in Mexico.

Langostina (lahn GOHS tee nah). Crayfish.

Lechón (leh CHON). Suckling pig. Cochinita is the word for suckling pig in the Yucatán Peninsula.

Lechuga (leh CHOO gah). Lettuce.

Legumbres (leh GOOM brehs). Vegetables. (See also *Verduras* below.)

Lengua (LEHN gwah). Tongue.

Lenguada (LEHN GWAH dah). Sole.

Lentaje (lehn TAH heh). Lentil.

Levadura (lay bah DOOH rah). Yeast.

Limón (lee MOHN). Lime. Lime juice gives an extra zip to soup and fish. Lime trees grow abundantly in Mexico so the fruit is cheap. Heaps of cut limes are as ubiquitous as salt and pepper on a Mexican dining table.

Lisa (LEE sah). Mullet.

Lomo (LOH moh). Loin.

Lomo Adobado (LOH moh ah doh BAH doh). Pork loin in a savory brown chile sauce. (See also *Adobo* above.)

Lonche (LOHN cheh). A specialty sandwich of Guadalajara. (See also Regional/Seasonal Specialties: *Lonche*.)

Longaniza (lohn gah NEE sah). Cured link sausage.

Macarrón (mah kah RROHN). Macaroni.

Machaca (mah CHAH kah). Beef that's been dried, salted, and shredded. (See also *Huevos* above.)

Maguey (MAH geh). Agave plant. There are many kinds of maguey in Mexico. One is used specifically for making the alcoholic drink known as pulque, another for tequila, still another for mezcal. The leaves are used in making a thin parchment paper used as a cooking wrapper for mixiotes and for lining earthen pits for cooking. A menu might mention something is wrapped in *hojas de maguey* (OH hahs deh MAH geh), meaning maguey leaves.

Maíz (mah EEZ). Corn. Another of Mexico's gifts to the world. The country's cuisine is still based on corn and peasants all over Mexico depend on their cornfields or *milpa* (MEEHL pah) to feed their families and their animals. This most basic of Mexican foods comes in white, yellow, and blue. Corn on the cob, however, is called *elote* (eh LOH teh). (See also *Elote* above and *Masa* below.)

Maizcena (mih ee SEH nah). Cornstarch.

Mamey (mah MEH). A delicious, slightly pear-flavored tropical fruit. The tan outer husk is broken to reveal an orangish interior.

Manchamanteles (mahn chah mahn TEH lehs). A sweet/picante mole. (See also *Mole* below and Regional/Seasonal Specialties: *Mole*.)

Mango (MAHN goh). Mango. Brought to Mexico after the Spanish Conquest, it's grown in plantations all along the coasts and in the interior. It's a relatively inexpensive fruit (compared to its price in the United States) and it's eaten fresh, in salads, and used in sauces with an international flare. Street vendors sculpt the juicy pulp into a tiered flower design and sell them on a stick with a flourish of ground chile and fresh lime juice.

Manitas (mah NEE tahs). Literally "little feet." It refers to feet used in cooking such as those of the pig, cow, or crab. Pickled pig's feet are offered as an appetizer and called simply manitas. (See also *Manitas de Cangrejo* below.)

Manitas de Cangrejo (mah NEE tahs deh kahn GREH hoh). The large fleshy claw of the stone crab. This delicacy is served with fresh lime or perhaps a little mayonnaise for added flavor, but almost never tartar sauce. Stone crabs are harvested off the coast of Campeche and Quintana Roo, both on the Yucatán Peninsula.

Manteca (mahn TEH kah). Lard. It's made from pig fat.

Mantequilla (mahn teh KEE yah). Butter. (See also *Margarina* below.)

Mantequilla de Cacahuate (mahn teh KEE yah deh caca WAH teh). Another way of saying peanut butter (also called *crema de cacahuate*).

Manzana (mahn ZAH nah). Apple. (See also Beverages A to Z: *Refresco*.)

Maple (MAH pleh). Maple syrup.

Margarina (mar gah REE nah). Margarine. *Mantequilla* (mahn teh KEE yah) is butter.

Mariscos (mah REEZ kohs). Seafood.

Masa (MAH sah). Ground cooked corn made into a smooth dough. Dried ground corn, mixed with lime slake, is formed into masa dough for use in making the daily quantity of tortillas. Masa is also the main ingredient of tamales. Though it translates as cornmeal dough it is not gritty and heavy as people from the United States are accustomed to thinking of cornmeal. Nor is something made from it heavily corn tasting.

To make the daily supply of tortillas, cooks once spent hours preparing the corn and then grinding it on special stones *(metates)* kept in the home. While some people still do that, more often the prepared masa is purchased from the local tortilla factory called *tortillería* (tohr tee yeh REE ah) and carried home in buckets. From that people make their daily tortillas. Dry masa flour is also packaged and sold in supermarkets. (See also Market Buying Tips: *Masa de Maíz / Masa de Harina.*)

Masa Harina (MAH sah hah REE nah). Corn flour.

Masa de Trigo (MAH sah deh TREE goh). Wheat flour.

Mayonesa (meh yoh NEH sah). Mayonnaise. Mexican mayonnaise is deliciously flavored with a hint of lime. (See Market Buying Tips: *Mayonesa.*)

Médula (MEH dooh lah). Bone marrow. It's also called *tuétano*. Mexican cooks create wonderful food using bone marrow. Bone marrow soup or *sopa de médula* (SOH pah deh MEH dooh lah) combines large pieces of soft white marrow with a seductively spiced (not picante) tomato and chile broth.

Mejorana (meh hoh RAH nah). Marjoram.

Melón (meh LOHN). Cantaloupe.

Membrillo (mehm BREE yoh). The fruit called quince.

Memela (meh MEH lah). An Oaxaca botana. (See Regional/Seasonal Specialties: *Botana.*)

Menta (MEHN tah). Mint.

Menudo (meh NOO doh). Tripe stew. Said to be a hangover remedy, it's popular on Saturday or Sunday mornings in Mexican markets. It's stomach meat, but has the disquieting smell of intestines and may be accompanied by pig's feet. It's prepared in a red broth with chorizo, onions, tomatoes, red chiles, and other spices. In northern Mexico it may be in a white broth and around Mexico City it's called *pancita* (pahn SEE tah). For those who have acquired the taste. (See also *Tripa* below, and Regional/Seasonal Specialties: *Menudo*.)

Mermilada (mehr MEE lah dah). Any kind of fruit preserve usually offered for toast or on pancakes.

Mero (MEHR roh). Grouper fish.

Miel (mee YEHL). Honey. Mexico's extensive honey production shows in the variety of honey cultivated countrywide. Cultivation is especially visible in the Yucatán Peninsula, where numerous honey hives can be seen from the highway. Ancient Maya had a god of honey they depicted on pyramids.

Migajas (mee GAH hahs). Crumbs.

Milanesa (mee lah NEH sah). Breaded steak. Inferior cuts of beef are pounded to a thin slab, and fried in an egg and bread batter. You never know when you'll win a steak as tough as a tire or one that cuts with a fork. Fresh limes and mayonnaise are served for flavoring and the meat is usually accompanied with beans, rice, and a small salad.

Mil Hojas (meel OH hahs). A rich cream puff which translates as "a thousand leaves." The light flaky pastry is filled with puffy cream and rolled in slivered white chocolate.

Mixiotes (mee SHOH tehs). Meat, either lamb, chicken, or rabbit, wrapped in parchment paper and steamed in a rich broth. (See Regional/Seasonal Specialties: *Mixiotes*.)

Mojarra (moh HAH rrah). The fish known as perch.

Mole (MOH leh). This most famous of Mexico's sauces is flavorful and complex with countless variations in striking colors—green, red, brown, black, yellow, and golden yellow. Its twenty to thirty disparate ingredients include ground tortillas, stale bread, pumpkin and sesame seeds, almonds, peanuts, raisins, cloves, peppercorns, a variety of chiles, vinegar, tomatoes, onion, garlic, and in some moles— but not all—a touch of chocolate. Typically this cherished sauce is ladled over turkey, chicken, or enchiladas and it's often included in tamales.

Some people love it, and others never acquire a taste for it, but everyone agrees it's best eaten at the noon meal, for complete digestion of its rich ingredients may require the remainder of the day.

The word mole comes from *mulli*, the Aztec word for sauce. It isn't certain if an Aztec sauce resembled this one or not, and there are a number of stories about the birth of the present sauce. The most frequently told tale, however, is that its inventor was a colonial-era nun in Puebla who was charged with preparing an honorable meal fit for a visit of the archbishop. Judging from the unusual combination and number of ingredients, it would seem that she emptied the cabinets in search of just the right high-drama taste for this sauce. She presented the exotic sauce, no doubt with a grand flourish, spread over turkey and dotted with sesame seeds—just as it appears today. The original Puebla-style mole or *mole poblano* (MOH leh poh BLAH noh) now has many robust cousins throughout the republic.

The red and green *pipián* (pee pee YAHN) sauces are also in the mole family, but their ingredients feature pumpkin or squash seeds paired with chiles, sesame, and other spices. Enhanced with fruit, Manchamanteles and Coloradito are two of the sweeter moles. Moles vary greatly in their heat quotient from sweet and mild to plenty spicy. (See also Regional/Seasonal Specialties: *Mole* and Market Buying Tips: *Mole* and *Pipián*.)

Molejas de Res (moh LEH hahs deh rehs). Veal sweetbreads.

Molletes (moh YEH tehs). A filling meal made with an opened *bolillo* (bohl EE yoh), a large white roll, spread with refried beans and topped with cheese that is broiled to melting. (Not to be confused with *molotes* [moh LOH tehs] described below.) Fresh salsa, added at the table, provides a sprightly zip. It's a particularly filling breakfast food, though it can usually be ordered throughout the day.

Molotes (moh LOH tehs). A very different kind of tortilla or *quesadilla* (kay sah DEE yah). (See also Regional/Seasonal Specialties: *Molotes.*)

Momocho (moh MOH cho). Another word for chicharrón. (See also *Chicharrón* above.)

Monguls (mohn GOOLS). A Hidalgo state specialty of marinated and baked pork rind. (See also Regional/Seasonal Specialties: *Monguls.*)

Morilla (moh REE yah). Morel mushroom.

Moronga (mohr OHN gah). Blood sausage.

Mostaza (mohs TAH sah). Mustard.

Muk Bil Pollo (mook BEEL POH yoh). An exotic pit-baked tamal made in the Yucatán during the Days of the Dead, November 1–2. (See also Regional/Seasonal Specialties: *Tamales/Muk Bil Pollo.*)

Nabo (NAH boh). Turnip.

Nance (NAHN seh). Chokecherry. A sweet yellow fruit.

Naranja (nah RAHN hah). Orange. Pyramid-shaped orange mounds are staples in the landscape of Mexican markets, and huge glasses of freshly squeezed orange juice are perks of south-of-the-border travel.

Naranja Agria (nah RAHN hah AH gree ah). Sour or bitter orange. This orange is as big as a small grapefruit, smells faintly like an orange, but tastes more like a lemon or lime. It's favored by cooks in marinades and sauces. Vinegar or a mixture of lime and orange juice may be substituted, although the naranja agria tree grows profusely in Mexico.

Nata (NAH tah). Thickened cream skimmed from boiled milk and mixed with sugar.

Natilla (nah TEE yah). A thick delicious pudding faintly flavored with vanilla.

Negro (NEH groh). Black. You'll see this describing the color of sauces, particularly in the Yucatán Peninsula.

Nieve (nee YEH beh). Fruit-flavored shaved ice. Pushcart vendors shout "nieve, nieve" on streets countrywide. They're selling shaved ice that's dished into cone-shaped cups and dribbled with thick, colorful fruit juices. It's a refreshing treat for the locals. But tourist beware—the blocks of ice they use are not made with purified water.

Nixtamal (neeks tah MAHL). Corn kernels softened in lime to remove outer skin in preparation for tortilla dough. (See also *Masa* above.)

Nogada (noh GAH dah). Walnuts or in a walnut sauce. (See also *Chiles en nogada* above.)

Nopales (noh PAH lehs). Nopal (prickly pear) cactus. Stripped of their thorns, the cactus pads are cut in strips and boiled as a vegetable, or combined with potatoes as you would green beans. Occasionally they are a choice to be scrambled into eggs at breakfast. A tangy salad mixes cooked nopales strips with onions, vinegar, oil, white cheese, cilantro, and spices.

Nuez (noo WEHS). Nut, usually pecan.

Olla (OH yah). Pot. The word is usually joined with something cooked or served in a clay pot.

Orégano (oh REH gah noh). Oregano. Mexican oregano, which grows upright and has purple flowers, has a different, milder, yet very oregano flavor than the low-growing, slightly hot *Origanum pulchellum* available in the United States.

Orejone (oh reh HOH neh). Romaine lettuce.

Ostión (ohs tee OHN). Oyster.

Palmito (pahl MEE toh). Hearts of palm.

Palomitas (pah loh MEE tahs). Popcorn.

Pambazo (pahm BAH soh). A sandwich that's dipped in a red sauce and fried. (See also Regional/Seasonal Specialties: *Pan/Pambazo.*)

Pámpano (PAHM pah noh). The fish pompano.

Pan (pahn). Bread. Mexico's cuisine features more than 500 different breads. But in restaurants, the choice usually boils down to three. To seek your preference for the meal, the waiter will often ask, "*¿Pan Bimbo* or *pan bolillo* or *tortilla?*" But others are sometimes offered as well.

- *Bimbo* (BEEM boh). Bimbo brand bread is the sliced white bread or *pan blanco* (pahn BLAN koh) of Mexico.
- *Bolillo* (boh LEE yoh). A large French-style roll served at almost all meals.
- *Pan dulce* (pahn DOOL say). Sweet bread. Mexico's repertoire of lightly sweet breads, rolls, and buns are largely descended from the French rule of Mexico in the 1860s. These lightly sweet breads come in a wide array of shapes including puffy rounds with shell designs on top, dusted with sugar, conical tubes stuffed with a sugar paste, croissant-like sweet rolls called *cuernos* (KWEHR nohs) for horns (which they resemble), to sweet small loaves called *panque* (PAHN keh) to . . . well, the assortment is enormous. Baskets of these are offered at breakfast in restaurants and bakeries called *panaderías* (pah nyah dah REE ahs) sell them all.
- *Pan Francés* (pahn frahn SEHS). French bread. On the breakfast menu it's the ubiquitous egg

batter–soaked fried bread that's served with syrup, honey, or marmalade. In a bakery it's the long loaves of French bread. As in most places outside France, Mexico's rendition of French bread looks like its French cousin, but it's denser.

- *Pan integral* (pahn en teh GRAHL). Whole wheat bread.
- *Pan de muerto* (pahn deh MWEHR toh). Special puffy and faintly sweet bread made for the November 1–2 Mexican holidays known as Days of the Dead. The commemorations are a cross between Halloween and Memorial Day.
- *Pan de yema* (pahn deh YEH mah). Egg yolk bread. (See also *Bolillo* above and *Tortilla* below, Regional/Seasonal Specialties: *Pan* and *Tortilla*, and Market Buying Tips: *Pan*.)
- *Tortilla* (tohr TEE yah). A flat bread that has been the basic bread of the country for thousands of years.

Pancita (pahn SEE tah). This is the word for menudo (tripe stew) in and around Mexico City. (See also *Menudo* above and Regional/Seasonal Specialties: *Menudo*.)

Panela (pah NEH lah). Unrefined brown sugar or a type of cheese. (See also *Piloncillo* and *Queso* below.)

Pan Molido (pahn moh LEE doh). Bread crumbs.

Panucho (pah NOO choh). A fried cornmeal appetizer. (See Regional/Seasonal Specialties: *Botana/Panuchos*.)

Panza (PAHN sah). Stomach.

Papa (PAH pah). Potato. (Besides those listed below, see also Regional/Seasonal Specialties: *Torta*.)

- Hash browns seldom find their way into Mexican restaurants. If they have them, the waiter may say, *"Tipo hash brown"* (TEE poh hash brown), meaning hash brown type. Savvy restaurants with a good breakfast menu will have them, as will large American-style chain restaurants in Mexico.
- *Papas francés* (PAH pahs frahn SEHS) are, of course, french fries.
- *Papas fritas* (PAH pahs FREE tahs) are fried potatoes, which could be sliced fried potatoes or french fries.
- *Papa al horno* (PAH pah ahl OHR noh). A baked potato.
- *Papa puré* (PAH pah poo REH). Mashed potatoes. Mexican mashed potatoes are silky smooth.
- *Papitas cambray* (pah PEE tahs KAHM breh). Tiny potatoes.

Papadzules (pah pahd SOO lehs). Corn tortillas stuffed with hard-boiled eggs, and topped with a savory green sauce. Ground squash seeds make the sauce and the dish is decorated with a stream of tomato sauce and crumbled boiled egg.

Papaya (pah PIH yah). The large papaya fruit grows in abundance in Mexico. Its meat is orange and the taste ranges from bland to sweet. Squeeze on fresh lime juice for a tangy accent.

Parrillada (pah ree YAH dah). A flame-grilled meat platter.

Pasa (PAH sah). Raisin.

Pasta (PAHS tah). Pasta. (See also Comfort Foods: Pasta.)

Pastel/Pasteles (pahs TEHL/pahs TEH lehs). Dessert, cake, or pastry. However, a pastel de pollo (pahs TEHL deh POH yoh), for example, would be a chicken pot pie, but a *pastel de chocolate* (pahs TAYL deh choh koh LAH teh) would be chocolate cake or some sort of sweet chocolate dessert. (See also *Postre* below, and Market Buying Tips: *Pan.*)

Pastes (PAHS tehs). Pasties, the English meat turnover. (See Regional/Seasonal Specialties: *Pastes.*)

Patas (PAH tahs). Feet. Nothing is wasted in Mexico, not even feet, when it comes to cooking. Though you might not detect the foot of a cow, *patas de res* (PAH tahs deh rehs), in your bowl or on a plate, the cook may have used it for flavor. You might see pig's feet, *manita* (mah NEE tah), which kindly translates as "little feet," on a menu or pickled in a bowl served as a condiment to flavor a meal. And chicken feet, *patas de pollo* (PAH tahs deh POH yoh), could bob unexpectedly in an authentic bowl of chicken soup, though more than likely the cook will remove them before serving. Chicken feet are said to impart a particularly rich flavor to soup. (See also *Manitas* above.)

Pato (PAH toh). Duck.

Pavo (PAH boh). Turkey. This feathery creature is native to Mexico and was introduced to the world after the Spanish conquest of Mexico. (See also *Guajolote* above and Regional/Seasonal Specialties: *Pavo.*)

Pay (pay). Pie.

Pechuga (peh CHOO gah). Breast.

Pellizcada (peh yeez KAH dah). A southern Veracruz-style tortilla. (See also Regional/Seasonal Specialties: *Tortilla.*)

Peneques (peh NEH kehs). A corn tortilla that's baked in a half-moon shape and is ready for stuffing with meat or cheese. It's dipped in egg white batter and fried, then adorned with a green or red sauce.

Pepino (peh PEE noh). Cucumber.

Pepita (peh PEE tah). The kernel of a pumpkin seed. It's sold dried, salted, and whole as a packaged snack, or dried and ground for use in many sauces.

Pera (PEH rah). Pear.

Perejil (peh reh HEEL). Parsley.

Pescado a la Talla (pehs KAH doh ah lah TAH yah). Delicious seasoned red snapper that's a specialty of Acapulco. (See also Regional/Seasonal Specialties: *Pescado a la Talla.*)

Pez Vela (pehs BEH lah). Sailfish.

Pibil (pee BEEL). A Yucatecan Mayan word for pit-baked, as in pollo and cochinita pibil.

Picada (pee KAH dah). A dish by the same name is two different things in Veracruz and Puebla. The word also means "chopped." (See also Regional/Seasonal Specialties: *Botana/Picada.*)

Picadillo (pee kah DEE yoh). The judiciously proportioned mixture of ground beef and pork, fried with tomatoes, onions, and peppers may also include dried fruits and almonds; it may be slightly sweet and it's not usually picante. Chiles rellenos are often stuffed with it and it's regularly included in breakfast buffets, and sometimes as a filling for tacos. (See also *Chile Relleno* above.)

Pichon (pee CHON). Pigeon.

Pico de Gallo (PEE koh deh GAH yoh). Literally, rooster's beak. The misappropriation of this word in the United States by using it to describe what in Mexico is salsa cruda (a tasty quartet of chopped tomatoes, cilantro, onions, and chile), muddies the waters for understanding what it is in Mexico.

If you order pico de gallo in Mexico you'll get an array of sliced oranges, jícama, and perhaps melon and cucumber arranged in the shape of a rooster's tail either served with fresh lime and chile powder or topped with shredded coconut. (Don't question this name of the rooster's beak versus presentation in the shape of a rooster's tail.) Occasionally these ingredients are made like a chopped salad and seasoned with salt and red pepper.

To further confuse the definition, a few restaurants catering to Americans will describe the contents of a Mexican plate meal and mention pico de gallo—meaning it's just like their clients know it at home and not like the real pico de gallo of Mexico! *Ay yi yi.* (See also *Salsa/Salsa Cruda* below.)

Pierna (pee YEHR nah). Leg.

Piloncillo (pee lohn SEE yoh). Unrefined hard brown sugar shaped into a cone and sold in Mexican markets.

Pimentón (pee mehn TOHN). Paprika or pimento pepper.

Pimienta Chica/Pimienta Negra (pee mee YEHN tah CHEE kah/NEH grah). Black peppercorn.

Pimienta Gorda (pee mee YEHN tah GOHR dah). Allspice berry.

Pimienta Morrone (pee mee YEHN tah moh RROH neh). Bell pepper.

Pimiento (pee mee YEHN toh). Pimento pepper.

Pimiento Rojo (pee mee EN toh ROH hoh). Red bell pepper.

Piña (PEEN yah). Pineapple. The cultivation of pineapple is thought to have arrived in Mexico by way of Brazil.

Pinchito (peen CHEE toh). Shish kebab.

Pinole (pee NOH leh). A dry mixture of roasted ground corn and brown sugar. Amaranth grains are also finely ground to make into pinole, which is sometimes used as a dusting on creamy pies. Pinch a dab of either and toss it in your mouth. Pinole is also used to make a hot, sweet, thick drink.

Piñón (peen YOHN). Pine nut.

Pipián (pee pee YAHN). A green or red mole featuring ground pumpkin or melon and sesame seeds paired with chiles and spices. (See also *Mole* above, Market Buying Tips: *Mole*, and Regional/Seasonal Specialties: *Pipián*.)

Pistache (pees TAH cheh). Pistachio.

Pitahaya (peet ah WAH yah). A tropical fruit. A pale red fruit with a sweet, pink pulp scattered with lots of black seeds.

Pizza (PEET sah). Pizza. The pies that swept the world come steaming from brick ovens all over Mexico. Crusts are excellent, but the topping flavors are not what you might expect due to different cheeses, meat, substitute spices, and a super-thin layer of plain tomato sauce. A standard cheese and mushroom pizza is hard to find, though that combination sometimes is an extra-cost option.

Plátano (PLAH tah noh). Banana. A rampant fruit in Mexico, the banana is believed to have arrived for cultivation in Mexico through Asia and Africa. There are at least three main varieties in Mexico. The first two can be peeled and eaten.

- *Plátano dedo* (PLAH tah noh DEH doh) or *plátano dominico* (PLAH tah noh doh mee NEE koh). Small, sweet, yellow, finger-sized eating bananas.
- *Plátano macho* (PLAH tah noh MAH choh). Plan-

tain. This one is used for cooking. It's a large banana, with a stout outer layer that's rather purple/green/yellow in color. The outer peel must turn black before the inner portion is suitable for cooking.

- *Plátano tabasco* (PLAH tah noh tah BAHS koh). The common yellow eating banana.

Platillo (plah TEE yoh). A platter of something. The word will be followed by the ingredients on the platter. Platón is another word for platter.

Plato surtido (PLAH toh soor TEE doh). An assortment or sampling of something; a combination plate. Appetizer portions of the menu often offer an assortment of the region's food, or appetizers, or perhaps a taste of regional meats.

Platón (plah TOHN). Platter.

Poblana(o) (poh BLAH nah/noh). Something prepared as it is in the city or state of Puebla would be called poblana (or poblano).

Poblano (poh BLAH noh). A large green chile. (See also *Chiles Frescos/Poblano* above.)

Poc Chuc (pohk CHOOK). Yucatán-style marinated grilled pork. (See also Regional/Seasonal Specialties: *Poc Chuc*.)

Pollo (POH yoh). Chicken. Certain chicken dishes that are regional specialties have crossed regional lines and are sometimes seen on menus far from their place of origin. Such is the case with the Yucatecan specialty of pollo pibil (POH yoh pee BEEL), which is pit-baked chicken seasoned with achiote preparado. *Pollo rostisado* (POH yoh rohs tee SAH doh) is roast chicken. Chickens roasting on revolving spits in restaurant windows beckon patrons all over the country. The practice of infusing the chicken with herbs or other flavors isn't done, but the meat is usually juicy and good. (See also Regional/Seasonal Specialties: *Pollo.*)

Pollo en Polvo (POH yoh ehn POHL boh). Chicken bouillon. Store-bought chicken bouillon is a cook's secret weapon for quick chicken stock, and the purchased variety is better in Mexico than in the United States.

Poro (POH roh). Leek. It's also called *puerro* (PWEHR roh).

Postre (POHS treh). Dessert. Dessert in Mexico ranges from uneventful, overly sturdy, gelatin to rich multilayerd cakes, crepes, tarts, pies, and ice cream. (See also *Dulce/Dulces* and *Pastel/Pasteles* above.)

Pozole (poh ZOH leh). A pork or chicken and hominy soup with condiments. A *pozoleria* (poh soh leh

REE ah) is a restaurant specializing in pozole. (See also Regional/Seasonal Specialties: *Pozole*.)

Puchero (pooh CHEH roh). A splendid stew. This salubrious gathering includes beef, lamb, and chicken simmered with corn, carrots, squash, garbanzos, cabbage, and sweet potatoes. Cooked bananas, pears, and peaches are added at serving. Puchero is also the name of a spice blend or *recado* (reh KAH doh) made of ground cloves, cinnamon, cumin, saffron, oregano, and black pepper.

Puerco (PWEHR koh). Pork. (See also *cerdo* above.)

Puerquitos (PWEHR KEE tohs). Hard cookies shaped in the form of a pig and made of brown sugar, lard, flour, and cinnamon.

Pulpo (POOL poh). Octopus. *Pulpo en su tinta* (POOL poh en sooh TEEN tah) is octopus in its ink.

Puntas de Filete (POON tahs deh fee LEH teh). Beef tips.

Quelites (keh LEE tehs). Lamb's-quarters, also known as goosefoot. Though quelites literally is lamb's-quarters (a weed to some people), it's often a word used to mean all kinds of greens. Spinach is a frequent substitute.

Quesadilla (keh sah DEE yah). A fried, stuffed tortilla. A flour tortilla (usually, but corn may be substituted) folded over white asadero or other good melting cheese and fried or warmed until the cheese is melted. One terrific version mixes cheese in the tortilla masa, which is then wrapped around more cheese and baked or fried. Often a leaf of epazote or serrano pepper is laid over the cheese and cooked inside the quesadilla. Though named for cheese (queso), quesadillas also hold fillings of meat, seafood, and potatoes, making them more like an empanada. (See also Regional/Seasonal Specialties: *Molotes* and *Quesadilla*.)

Queso (KEH soh). Cheese. Cheese and cheese making came to Mexico with the arrival of the Spanish, who brought cows and goats. The art of cheese making is a specialty in most parts of Mexico, and many people make their own cheese at home. Cheeses sold in markets and stores are a delicious and varied lot. In many cases, even though they are known by their regional name, the most popular regional cheeses can be found in, and are used in, most parts of the country. Except for a few cheeses, such as the *queso criollo* (kree OH yoh) of Taxco, which is similar to a Muenster cheese, and the hard, yellow Chihuahua cheese, most Mexican cheese is white. U.S.-style cottage cheese isn't sold in Mexico and there's no real equivalent. Note: Most Mexican cheese is not pasteurized.

- *Anejo* (ah NEH hoh). Aged (anejo) cheese is salty and sharp, similar to Romano cheese. Anejo is easily crumbled for casting over quesadillas and enchiladas.

- *Asadero* (ah sah DEH roh). A mild cheese, similar to mozzarella, used in quesadillas and other dishes for its melting quality.
- *Chihuahua/Mennonita*. Cheddar-like yellow cheese. Though it originated in the Mennonite communities near Chihuahua in northern Mexico, now it's created by Mennonites and non-Mennonites in other parts of Mexico.
- *Cotija* (koh TEE hah). A semi-strong-tasting crumbly goat cheese. Cotija cheese originated in Cotija, Michoacán, but the cheese is used all over Mexico.
- *Panela* (pah NEH lah). A smooth, softish cheese used sliced as a botana.
- *Quesillo* (keh SEE yoh). Rope cheese made in Oaxaca. Popular for its melting quality in quesadillas, in chiles rellenos, and as a soup topping. The long strands of quesillo are rolled into a ball resembling a ball of twine.
- *Queso de Cabra* (KEH soh deh KAH brah). Strong-tasting, crumbly goat cheese. Its taste is faintly that of blue cheese.
- *Queso Canasta* (KEH soh kah NAHS tah). The same as panela. It bears the imprint of the basket or canasta in which it's made.
- *Queso Criollo* (KEH soh kree OH yoh). Found in Taxco, Guerrero, it's a pale yellow cheese that looks and tastes similar to Muenster cheese.
- *Queso Fresco* (KEH soh FREHS koh). A spongy

cheese that can be like a mild feta. It's sometimes salty, and is used crumbled on botanas, tacos, and enchiladas, or sliced and served as a delicious accompaniment to the overly sweet ates (sugared fruit pastes) that are so popular for dessert.

- *Queso Parmesano* (KEH soh pahr meh SAH noh) is Parmesan cheese, but only the finest restaurants offer the real thing.
- *Requesón* (reh keh SOHN). A ricotta-like cheese. Delicious and low fat, it resembles ricotta cheese in texture, but it's milder in taste. It's used in enchiladas and quesadillas.

A May wine and cheese fair is held annually in Tequisquiapan, Querétaro, to celebrate the production of both commodities in that region. (See also entries for *queso* in Regional/Seasonal Specialties and Market Buying Tips.)

Queso Fundido (KEH soh foon DEE doh). White cheese melted in a pottery bowl (usually) and served with fresh hot flour tortillas for scooping and eating the cheese from the bowl.

Quintoniles (keen toh NEEL ehs). Cooked greens.

Rábano (RAH bah noh). Radish. It's used in salads and as one of several condiments to be dropped into pozole (pork or chicken and hominy soup) at the table. On Night of the Radishes or *Noche de los Rábanos* (NOH cheh deh lohs RAH bah nohs), December 23 in Oaxaca, the central plaza fills with displays of enormous carved radishes. A particular variety of radish that grows a foot or more in length and is larger than a fifty-cent piece around is grown by the city especially for carvers who enter this festival. They create enormous religious and secular scenes entirely out of these radishes.

Rajas (RAH hahs). Slices. Often used to refer to slices of chile pepper or grilled green onions.

Rallado (rah YAH doh). Grated.

Rama/Ramita (RAH mah/rah MEE tah). Sprig. It could refer to a sprig of any herb or plant.

Ranchero/Ranchera (rahn CHEH roh/rahn CHEH rah). Anything ranchero or ranchera will be in a mild tomato sauce with onions and chiles, such as *huevos rancheros* or *costillas rancheras*.

Rebanada (reh bah NAH dah). A slice of something, such as pizza or cake or bread.

Receta (reh SEH tah). Recipe.

Relleno (reh YEH noh). Stuffed.

Requesón (reh keh SOHN). A ricotta-like cheese. (See also *Queso* above.)

Res (REHS). Beef. Beef also goes by the name of *carne de res* (KAHR neh deh rehs) and *carne de vaca* (KAHR neh deh BAH kah). (See also *Carne* and *Bif* above.)

Riñones (reen YOH nehs). Kidneys.

Róbalo (ROH bah loh). Sea bass.

Rojo/Roja (ROH hoh/ROH hah). Red. Rojo or roja will be used to describe the color of a sauce, a broth, or the color of a chile, etc.

Rollo (ROH yoh). Roll.

Romerito (roh meh REE toh). This green vegetable looks like rosemary but is completely different in taste and rather bland by comparison. (See also Regional/Seasonal Specialties: *Romeritos*.)

Rosca de Reyes (ROHS kah deh REH yehs). A cake served on Epiphany, January 6. It's shaped like a large wreath and baked with a tiny china doll inside. Whoever gets the piece with the doll (which symbolizes the infant Christ) throws a party on Candlemas Day, February 2. Fancy roscas can occupy a huge dining table and be adorned with pastry flowers and incredible designs of nuts, fruits, and icing.

Sábalo (SAH bah loh). The fish called shad.

Sábana (SAH bah nah). A thin cut of beef. (See also Regional/Seasonal Specialties: *Sábana*.)

Salada (sah LAH doh). Salty. A waiter may mention that a food is salada.

Salmón (sahl MOHN). Salmon.

Salpicón (sahl pee KOHN). Shredded marinated beef. (See Regional/Seasonal Specialties: *Salpicón*.)

Salsa (SAHL sah). Fresh sauce made of chopped or blender-mixed ingredients. Usually presented in bowls to be added to food after serving.

- *Salsa cruda* (SAHL sah KROO dah). Misnamed as *pico de gallo* (PEE koh deh GAH yoh) in the United States. It combines small pieces of chopped fresh tomatoes, white onions, serrano or jalapeño peppers, and cilantro.
- *Salsa roja* (SAHL sah ROH hah). Blender-made salsa using fresh roasted tomatoes, chipotle peppers, garlic, and sometimes bits of cilantro.
- *Salsa verde cruda* (SAHL sah BEHR deh KROO dah). Blender-made, or hand-ground green sauce using *tomate verde* (toh MAH teh BEHR deh), which is a hard green tomato-like vegetable in a husk, serrano chiles, garlic, and white onion. Chunks of fresh avocado may be added at serving.

Salsa de Chicharrón (SAHL sah deh chee cha RROHN). Served as a main course, it's a large piece of pork rind cooked and served in a red sauce. It's not at all like the salsas described above. (See also Regional/Seasonal Specialties: *Salsa de Chicharrón*.)

Salsa Inglesa (SAHL sah een GLEH sah). Worcestershire sauce.

Salvia (SAHL bee yah). Sage.

Sandía (sahn DEE ah). Watermelon.

Sangre (SAHN greh). Blood. The word is used to describe something cooked in its own blood, or perhaps blood sausage.

Seco (SEH koh). Dry. The word may be used to describe wine, bread, meat, chiles, or a serving of plain rice.

Semilla (seh MEE yah). Seed.

Serrano (seh RAH noh). A hot, slender green chile pepper. (See also *Chiles Fresco* above.)

Sesos (SEH sohs). Brains. Mexicans serve brain tacos, brain stew, etc.

Seta (SEH tah). Mushroom. Hongo and champiñón are other words for mushroom.

Sierra (see YEH rah). Spanish mackerel.

Sopa (SOH pah). Soup. Mexicans excel at making soups, which vary dramatically from region to region. Fresh ingredients are the norm and only occasionally will the kitchen resort to *lata* (LAH-tah), meaning canned variety.

Most confusing to foreigners is the one called *sopa de arroz* (SOH pah deh AH roz), which literally means rice soup—but it's not soup. The word for rice listed on menus under soups has surprised many a tourist anticipating a brothy rice soup. Instead, a plate of plain white rice known as sopa de arroz appears, which is also called *sopa seca* (SOH pah SEH kah) or dry soup.

Soups are almost always accompanied by fresh lime slices, which when dribbled on soup give it an extra zip. Here are a few of the most common soups served countrywide.

- *Sopa Azteca* (SOH pah ahz TEH kah). A soup featuring thin fried tortilla strips. (See also *Sopa de tortilla* below.)
- *Sopa de elote* (SOH pah deh eh LOH teh). Corn soup. Another robust favorite that's usually thick and flavorful.
- *Sopa de fideo* (SOH pah deh fee DEH oh). Pasta soup. It's made of vermicelli or some other pasta in a tomato broth.
- *Sopa de Lima* (SOH pah deh LEE mah). Lime soup that's a specialty of the Yucatán Peninsula.

- *Sopa de médula* (SOH pah deh MEH doo lah). Bone marrow soup. (See also *Tuétano* below.)

- *Sopa de menudencias* (SOH pah deh meh noo DEN see yahs). Chicken intestine soup—with an aroma a la chicken coop.

- *Sopa Tlalpeño* (SOH pah tlahl PEH nyoh). Vegetable soup from Tlalpán, now a southern suburb of Mexico City. Long ago it blossomed beyond Tlalpán to appear in restaurants all over the country. This hearty soup should hold a handful of shredded chicken, a sprinkling of rice, carrots, and hominy, a few chunks of avocado, a few slivers of chile (not picante), a bit of fresh garlic, onions, cilantro, and tomato, all simmered together in a light chicken or beef stock. Though originally an inspired soup, sopa Tlalpeño may also be just another word for vegetable soup, without all the traditional ingredients.

- *Sopa de tortilla* (SOH pah deh tohr TEE yah). Tortilla soup, also known as *sopa Azteca*, a stalwart staple soup at the Mexican table. It's a nourishing chicken broth–based soup flavored with tomatoes, onion, garlic, and chiles. Sometimes there's such a tangle of crispy fried thin tortilla strips bobbing in the bowl that one must somehow plunge through them to get at the soup. It's laced with white cheese, thick cream, and perhaps a bit of fresh chopped cilantro.

- *Sopa xóchitl* (SOH pah SOH chee tl). This brothy soup can startle the unwary with its featured sliced serrano peppers floating on top. *Xóchitl* is the Aztec word for flower, and perhaps at one time flowers figured in this brew—but no more. Now its firepower is aimed at innocent diners who suspect nothing so hot could lurk in this harmless-looking broth.

- *Sopa de zanahoria* (SOH pah deh sah nah HOH ree ah). Carrot soup. One of the best soups in Mexico, made either with a broth base and carrots or with cream added.

Some soups or souplike dishes are also accompanied by other table-added condiments such as fresh chopped onions, cilantro, chopped serrano peppers, lettuce, cabbage, radishes, and dried oregano, to toss in according to individual tastes. (See also *Arroz, Birria, Caldo, Consomé,* and *Pozole* above and Regional/Seasonal Specialties: *Sopa, Birria,* and *Pozole*.)

Sopapilla (soh pah PEE yah). A fried fritter doused in sugar or honey that's called a *buñuelo* in Mexico.

Sope (SOH peh). A fried cornmeal botana. (See also *Botanas* above and Regional/Seasonal Specialties: *Botana*.)

Spaghetti (ehs pah GHEH tee). The menu spelling will be spaghetti, but the waiter will pronounce it the way it's spelled in Spanish—*espageti*. Well-flavored, authentic-tasting Italian food is hard to find in Mexico; nevertheless it's a stalwart on menus.

Taco (TAH koh). Soft corn or flour tortillas filled with meat or other combinations such as potatoes and *chorizo* (choh REEZ oh), or potatoes and eggs. Crispy tacos, those half-moon-shaped shells, invented and sold in the United States, aren't served in Mexico. Roll your own tacos in Mexico by placing the chopped meat or other filling into the tortillas, which are pulled fresh and hot from a covered basket. Assorted condiments for building your own tacos include grilled green onions, sliced white onions, chopped tomatoes, and cilantro.

- *Tacos al carbón* (TAH kos ahl kahr BOHN). Meat grilled over charcoal.
- *Tacos dorados* (TAH kos doh RAH dohs). A deep-fried taco. Flour or corn tortillas are stuffed with a filling (usually chicken) and then deep-fried. It's the same as a flauta. A small taco dorado is called a *taquito* (tah KEEH toh) when it's served as an appetizer. (See also *Flautas* above, *Taquitos* below, and Regional/Seasonal Specialties: *Tacos*.)
- *Tacos al pastor* (TAH kos ahl pahs TOHR). Delectable layers of pork revolving on a heated cylinder dripping with the juice of a fresh pineapple. In some places these are called *tacos arabe* (TAH kohs AH rah beh).

Tamal (tah MAHL). In this pre-Hispanic food, corn masa (dough) is stuffed with meat or cheese or with a sweet filling, wrapped in a corn husk, corn leaf, banana leaf, or other leafy wrapper, and steamed. Tamal (not tamale) is the word for one and *tamales* (tah MAH lehs) means more than one. The wrapper isn't eaten. (See Regional/Seasonal Specialties: *Tamales*.)

Tamarindo (tah mah REEN doh). Tamarind. Seeds of the tamarind tree are produced in a long brown husk. Though tart as a seed, when ground and blended with sugar and water they make a delightful agua fresca. When sugar is added to ground tamarind seeds, the result is an ate, an outrageously sweet dessert paste. Tamarind-flavored sauces are also making their way into alta cocina Méxicana. (See also *Ate* above.)

Tampiqueña (TAHM pee kehn yah). Something from the Gulf Coast city of Tampico or a meat prepared in the style of the Tampico Club in Mexico City.

Taquitos (tah KEE tohs). Tightly rolled corn tortillas stuffed with chicken and deep-fried. It's a flauta or taco dorado by another name except that a taquito is smaller and often served as a botana to accompany beer or alcoholic drinks. (See also *Flautas* and *Tacos dorados* above.)

Tasajo (tah SAH hoh). A thin, dried piece of beef that's a specialty of Oaxaca and Chiapas. (See also *Cecina* above.)

Taza / Tazón (TAH sah / tah SOHN). Cup / large cup.

Tepesquintle (teh pehs KWEENT leh). A plant-eating rodent featured in restaurants specializing in pre-Hispanic food. The reddish meat is a bit stringy, but it looks and tastes like roast beef.

Ternera (tehr NEH rah). Veal.

Tik-n-xic (teek en CHEEK). Grilled red snapper flavored with achiote. (See also Regional/Seasonal Specialties: *Tik-n-xic*.)

Tinga (TEEN gah). A special stew from the state of Puebla. (See Regional/Seasonal Specialties: *Tinga*.)

Tlacoyos (tlah KOH yohs). A canoe-shaped cornmeal appetizer. (See also *Antojitos* and *Chalupa* above.)

Tocino (toh SEEN oh). Bacon. It's usually fresh and served in generous portions.

Tomate Rojo (toh MAH teh ROH hoh). Red tomato also called *jitomate* (heeh toh MAH teh).

Tomate Verde (toh MAH teh BEHR deh). A hard green tomato-like fruit wrapped in a thin paper husk. It's also called a tomatillo and it's used in combination with green chiles in making green sauces. Red tomatoes are called *jitomate* (heeh toh MAH teh.)

Tomatillo (toh mah TEE yoh). This is another word for the tomate verde (toh MAH tay BEHR deh).

Tomillo (toh MEE yoh). Thyme.

Topotes (toh POH tehs). Tiny dried/fried fish that are similar to charales. (See also Regional/Seasonal Specialties: *Charales.*)

Toronja (toh ROHN hah). Grapefruit.

Torta (TOHR tah). What a sandwich is called in Mexico. Or it can be a dessert. You'll know by its placement on the menu. As a sandwich, it's usually made with a bolillo roll. Sometimes it's served with fresh cold ingredients of meat, avocado, tomato, and cheese. The bread may be spread with mayonnaise or fresh thick cream. But Mexicans seem to favor a warm sandwich, so the meat and bun are fried or warmed on a grill first and the whole sandwich is served warm—making the tomato, lettuce, and avocado a bit limp. Other uses for the word torta have no association with a sandwich or a dessert, and there are regional sandwiches that aren't called tortas! (See Regional/Seasonal Specialties: *Torta, Pambazo, Chanclas, Cemitas,* and *Lonche.*)

Tortilla (tohr TEE yah). A round corn or wheat flour flat bread.

For thousands of years, the tortilla has figured as a staple in the Mexican diet. Wheat flour tortillas are a northern Mexico specialty, though they're found outside the north. Corn tortillas, made with yellow, white, and blue corn are the most frequently offered outside the north. Piles of freshly made tortillas are served at most meals that feature Mexican food. In restaurants the waiter/waitress will exchange lukewarm tortillas for hot fresh ones without being asked. Good and hot is how they're eaten.

There's a bit of etiquette to eating tortillas. Mexican's forgive foreigners for spreading tortillas with butter, something a Mexican isn't likely to do. It's perfectly polite to roll the versatile disk into a loose tube and use it as a pusher or scooper—good for chasing beans around a plate, or for shepherding other errant victuals onto a fork. Diners hold the rolled tortilla in the left hand and take bites of the scooper with the meal. When the tortilla is gone, they roll another. And finally, to look like a knowledgeable native, you'll want to eat on the correct side of your tortilla. Tortillas often have one side with a broken bubble where the tortilla puffed up and broke during cooking, leaving a torn bit of tortilla—that side goes inside. Otherwise it dangles to demonstrate that you're eating on the wrong side of the tortilla.

The versatile tortilla has many personalities. It's an edible plate when turned into a taco, chalupa, flauta, or tostada. Leftover tortillas turn up in chilaquiles and tortilla soup. Cut in triangular-shaped wedges and baked or fried, these crispy pieces are called totopos and stand like stout sentries in a mound of frijoles refritos and guacamole salad where they're to be used instead of a fork and eventually consumed. Except in Acapulco, crispy fried tortillas are the staple attendant to a plate of fresh ceviche. In market cookshops, when tortillas will do as a utensil, a fork isn't supplied.

Though many people still make their tortillas at home (handmade is considered superior to machine made), lines of clients form outside *tortillerias* (tortilla factories) to buy them ready made by the kilo. If made at home, a special press is used to make corn tortillas; while flour tortillas are still formed by hand. (See also Regional/Seasonal Specialties: *Tortilla*.)

Tostada (tohs TAH dah). A fried-to-a-crisp, flat corn tortilla, piled high with any combination of beans, meat, cheese, avocados, lettuce, and tomato. The word also is used in toasted bread or *pan tostado* (pahn tohs TAH doh). It also refers to small, plain, baked tortillas served with ceviche. *Bien tostada* (bee YEHN tohs TAH dah) means well toasted or crisp. (See also *Chalupa* above.)

Totopo (toh TOH poh). A hard tortilla, whole or cut in a wedge, used to scoop guacamole, refried beans, or ceviche. (See also Regional/Seasonal Specialties: *Tortilla* and *Botana*.)

Trigo (TREE goh). Wheat. The Spaniards introduced wheat to Mexico.

Tripa (TREE pah). Tripe. Animal stomach. *Callos* (KAH yohs), its name in Spain, is sometimes used. (See also *Menudo* and *Pancita* above.)

Trucha (TROO chah). Trout.

Tuétano (too EH tah noh). Bone marrow. (See also *Médula* above.)

Tuna (TOO nah). Red or green fruit of the prickly pear cactus. It's turned into agua fresca and sweet desserts, as well as eaten fresh.

Uchepo (ooh CHEH poh). A Michoacán-style tamal. (See Regional/Seasonal Specialties: *Tamales*.)

Uva (OOH bah). Grape.

Uva de Corinto (OOH bah deh koh REEN toh). Currant.

Vaca (BAH kah). Cow. Cattle were unknown in Mexico before being introduced by the Spanish conquerors. The word may be used to describe which milk is used in a cheese, or what animal was used as meat in a dish.

Vainilla (by NEE yah). Vanilla. Native to Mexico and grown around Papantla in northern Veracruz.

Vegetal (beh heh TAHL). Vegetable. (See also *Verduras* below and *Legumbres* above.)

Venado (beh NAH doh). Venison.

Verde (BEHR deh). Green. Verde will be used to describe the color of a sauce, a broth, or a chile, etc.

Verdolaga (BEHR doh LAH gah). Purslane or *portulaca oleracea*, also known as moss rose. It's eaten fresh in salads, and used in stews and green mole.

Verduras (BEHR DOOH rahs). Cooked vegetables. (See also *Legumbres* above.)

Vinagre (beeh NAH greh). Vinegar.

Vinagreta (beeh nah GREH tah). Viniagrette.

Vuelva a la Vida (BWEHL bah ah lah BEEH dah). Literally, this means "back to life." A dish named this will be a large seafood cocktail in a mild tomato sauce.

Waffle (WAHF leh). Waffle. It's spelled as it is in English and means the same thing as the breakfast waffle, but it's pronounced differently.

Yema de Huevo (YEH mah deh WEH boh). Egg yolk.

Yucca (YOO kah). A root. White and potato-like in consistency, but richer in flavor than a potato, it's eaten most by coastal communities either boiled or fried. Yucca fritters turn the root into a fried dessert mixed with sugar, eggs, and cinnamon.

Zacahuil (sah kah WEEL). A Veracruz-style tamal. (See Regional/Seasonal Specialties: *Tamales*.)

Zanahoria (zah nah HOH ree yah). Carrot. Carrots appear in potato salad and as a delicious soup.

Zapote (sah POH teh). Zapote. A vitamin-rich, tropical fruit with several different colors of pulp, including black. Black zapote is sweet, and the consistency is rather like canned cranberry that can be eaten with a spoon.

Zarzamora (sahr zah MOH rah). Blackberry.

BEVERAGES A TO Z

· ▦ ·

Mᴇxɪᴄᴏ's ᴅɪɴɪɴɢ tradition includes a robust variety of beverages from fruit-flavored water and soft drinks, to stout and mild beer, rum, tequila, and brandy, and lightly fermented drinks handed down from pre-Hispanic times. Mexican-produced liquor is a much less expensive choice than any imported brand on which there are high import taxes.

As a precautionary hint, in Mexico canned drinks (beer, juice, and soft drinks) are transported over many dusty roads before reaching their destination. So it's best to at least thoroughly wipe clean the top of a can or bottle before opening or drinking from it. Or you can use a straw or transfer the contents to a glass. However, use of a glass in market fondas isn't recommended since it probably won't have been washed in hot water. In that case use a straw in canned and bottled drinks bought in a market fonda.

Another precaution should be in the use of ice, which is safe only if it is made from purified water.

(For how to ask about ice, see also Menu Primer A to Z: *Hielo*.)

Below are some of the highlights of drinking in Mexico.

Nonalcoholic Drinks

Agua (AHG wah). Water. Purified bottled water produced in Mexico is sold widely in pharmacies, groceries, liquor stores, and almost any abarrote. Imported brands such as Evian are extremely expensive. A few top hotels provide purified tap water but continue to place bottles of purified water in the room. These hotels sometimes charge guests for using the bottled water, especially if it's an imported brand. Restaurants catering to tourists may also fill guest glasses from a pitcher carried to the table. It's understood that this is purified water. But when in doubt ask if it's purified: "*¿Es purificado?*" (ehs pooh reeh fee KAH doh). As a general rule, however, stick with bottled purified water.

- *Agua dulce* (AHG wah DOOL seh). Fresh water, although literally translated it means sweet water. The term is used to differentiate drinking water from saltwater or *agua salada* (ahg wah sahl AH dah).
- *Agua filtrado* (AHG wah feel TRAH doh). Filtered water. Filters generally do not filter out all impurities, so avoid it.
- *Agua con gas* (AHG wah kohn gahs). Carbonated bottled mineral water.

- *Agua sin gas* (AHG wah seen gahs). Uncarbonated water bottled like a soft drink.
- *Agua purificada* (AHG wah pooh reeh fee KAH dah). Purified water. It comes in plastic containers in various sizes from purse totable to giant.

Aguas frescas (AHG wahs FREHS kahs). Literally translated it means "fresh waters," but in practice pureed fresh fruit is mixed with water and ice creating a refreshing drink. Just be sure the water and ice are purified. (Besides those listed below, see also Market Buying Tips: *Aguas Frescas.*)

- *Agua de chía* (AHG wah deh CHEE ah). Lemonade-like drink made with chía seeds, which float on top.
- *Agua de jamaica* (AHG wah deh hah MIH kah). Made with the dried part of an obscure flower and sugar.
- *Agua sandía* (AHG wah sahn DEE ah). Features watermelon.
- *Horchata* (hohr CHA tah). Made with either ground rice or ground cantaloupe seeds, cinnamon, and sugar.

Atole (ah TOH leh). A delicious, warm, and thick pre-Hispanic drink made of ground rice or finely ground cornmeal mixed with sugar. Ground pumpkin seeds are sometimes used. Vanilla and fresh flavors such as strawberries, bananas, pineapple, or other fruit are also sometimes added. Traditionally it's served in the evening or early morning as an accompaniment to tamales or sweet roles. The Aztecs called this warming drink *atulli*, and the Spanish pronunced it "ah TOH leh" and changed the spelling. Atole with cinnamon and chocolate added is called *champurrado* (chahm pooh RAH doh). *Atole de pepita* (ah TOH leh deh peh PEE tah), though not widely served, is made from ground pumpkin seeds. (See also *Champurrado* below.)

Café (kah FEH). Coffee.

- *Café Americano* (kah FEH ah mehr ree KAH noh). Black coffee.
- *Café con leche* (kah FEH kohn LEH cheh). Coffee with hot milk.
- *Café negro* (kah FEH NEH groh). The same as café Americano.
- *Café de olla* (kah FEH deh OH yah). A favorite of Mexicans is brewed coffee with cinnamon, sugar, and sometimes cloves added before serving.
- *Café Piquete* (kah FEH PEE KEH teh). Coffee laced with brandy.
- *Nescafé con café* (NEHS kah FEH kohn kah FEH). Coffee with a Mexican twist. A tablespoon of instant Nescafé is mixed into a glass of scalding hot milk for a surprisingly tasty form of coffee.

Coffee was introduced to Mexico by the Spaniards via a centuries-old route starting in Ethiopia. Today Mexico ranks third in the world in the export of coffee (behind Brazil and Colombia). Grown in Veracruz, Chiapas, Oaxaca, Puebla, Guerrero, and Hidalgo, some of the best known are found in Chiapas, and the Veracruz towns of Coatepec and Córdoba.

In San Cristóbal de las Casas, Chiapas patrons of the town's small coffeehouses play endless rounds of dominoes. But perhaps Veracruz is the town with the most prominent coffee tradition. In the city's large coffeehouses waiters scurry about carrying two kettles, one of scalding hot milk and the other of espresso. To summon the waiter patrons tap their glasses with spoons creating a constant coffeehouse chime. When the waiter arrives, the patron indicates the proportion of coffee to milk, which the waiter obliges, often showing his theatrical prowess at managing long streams of liquid flowing between kettles and glass.

Elsewhere in Mexico espresso machines pump out the ingredients for a variety of coffees and are found in most places frequented by tourists. However, the cold coffee rage hasn't quite caught on, though a few places excel at these and many other coffee concoctions.

Despite Mexico's own fine coffee, many restaurants offer only instant coffee. Decaffeinated coffee is slowly making its way into Mexico's restaurants; however, most decaffeinated coffee is instant.

Free coffee refills are occasionally served at restaurants having tourist savvy, but more often there's a charge for each cup consumed. (See also Market Buying Tips: *Café*).

Champurrado (cham poo RRAH doh). Chocolate atole. It should have a nice hint of cinnamon otherwise you've just been served hot chocolate—it happens. (See also *Atole* above.)

Coco Fresco (KOH koh FREHS koh). Fresh coconut milk. Sellers of this treat whack off the top of the coconut, pop a straw in the hole, and serve the beverage right in its original container. Often the coconuts are chilled so the drink is especially refreshing.

Horchata (hor CHA tah). Ground melon seed or rice drink. (See also *Aguas Frescas* above.)

Jugo (HOO goh). Juice. Juice bars all over the country feature fresh blended fruit drinks that are prepared from fresh fruit while you wait—and watch. Bellying up to one of Mexico's plentiful bars is one of the pleasures of traveling in a country that grows an enormous variety of tropical fruits—pineapple, banana, watermelon, guayaba, zapote, and mango, for example. Most juice bars will blend any combination of fruits any way you want them.

- *Jugo de naranja* (HOO goh deh nah RAHN hah). Orange juice.

- *Jugo de papaya* (HOO goh deh pah PAH yah). Papaya juice.
- *Jugo de piña* (HOO goh deh PEEN nyah). Pineapple juice.
- *Jugo de tomate* (HOO goh deh toh MAH teh). Tomato juice. It may be canned rather than freshly made.
- *Jugo de toronja* (HOO goh deh toh ROHN hah). Grapefruit juice.

Leche (LEH cheh). Milk. A glass of milk is *vaso de leche* (BAH soh deh LEH cheh).

Limonada (lee moh NAH dah). Lemonade. It will be made from freshly squeezed limes.

Liquada (lee KWAH dah). A blended fruit drink. It's made by combining various fruits together or with water or milk and sometimes yogurt. If it's made from water, make sure only purified water, *agua purificada* (AHG wah pooh ree fee KAH dah) has been used. (See also *Jugo* and *Agua* above.)

Pinole (pee NOH leh). Toasted cornmeal mixed with *piloncillo* (pee lohn SEE yoh), which is raw brown sugar ground into a fine powder. It's served as a hot drink, or pinches of the powder alone can be tossed into the mouth.

Ponche (POHN cheh). Fruit punch. A much-favored steaming hot festival drink, ponche is so chock full of large wedges of apples, pears, and pineapple that there's often little of the sweet liquid to savor. At some festivals, such as Days of the Dead at Mixquic (south of Mexico City), the brew is laced with rum. In Oaxaca at Christmastime, next to the cathedral, ponche is served with buñuelos with a stick of fresh sugarcane to stir and scoop out the tasty cooked fruit.

Refresco (reh FREHS koh). Soft drink. Besides the soft drinks known round the world such as Coca-Cola, Pepsi, Sprite, and 7-Up, which are widely sold in Mexico, a refreshing, apple-flavored carbonated drink is also sold by names that are a variant of *manzana* (mahn ZAH nah), which means apple. Just ask for manzana, or the brand name *Sidral* (see DRAHL), and the waiter or clerk will know. *Toronja* (toh ROHN hah), which is Spanish for grapefruit, is also used in energizing soft drinks and tastes similar to any brand or flavor using lemons or lime; it's used heavily in soft drinks.

Every small town, roadside stand, corner grocery and restaurant in Mexico sells cold soft drinks. Sales of these fuel the sugar industry in Mexico. Diet soft drinks are becoming more easily found, but may still be frustratingly absent in many places, including restaurants. Where bottled soft drinks are sold at a corner grocery called an *aborrote* (ah boh RROH teh), for example, you'll be charged for the bottle if you leave with it. Thus, clerks will often ask if you're taking the bottle and offer to save you money by pouring the liquid into a fresh plastic bag. The patron departs clutching the efficient neck of the bag with a straw protruding from the opening. Canned refrescos are also sold, but may be more expensive than those in bottles.

Té (teh). Tea. Black tea *té negro* (teh NEH groh), and chamomile tea, called *manzanilla* (mahn zah NEE yah) in Mexico, are the two most common teas offered. Only the most sophisticated restaurants *may* offer herbal tea or a variety of teas from around the world. Only a few of these top-notch restaurants will offer decaffeinated tea.

Té Helado (teh eh LAH doh). Iced tea. A few restaurants in heavily touristed areas have adopted the practice of providing free ice tea refills. Ordinarily free ice tea refills are uncommon.

Alcoholic Drinks

Aguardiente (ah gwahr dee YEHN teh). A potent alcohol made from distilled sugarcane.

Brandy. Brandy. Pronounced the same in English as in Spanish. Good Mexican brandies to select include Presidente, Solera, Fundador, and Don Pedro.

Cerveza (SEHR BEH sah). Beer. The excellent beers brewed in Mexico have a cult following among foreigners. Though a kind of beer was produced in Mexico as early as the mid-1500s, the industry didn't begin to flourish until the late 1800s when Cervecería Cuauhtémoc of Monterrey, and Cervecería Moctezuma, of Orizaba, Veracruz, began production. Cervecería Modelo came along in 1925, establishing its plant in Mexico City. This trio still produces fine Mexican beer.

- *Bohemia* (boh HEH mee ah). A top-quality light bottled beer.
- *Carta Blanca* (KAR tah BLAHN kah). Found most often in northern Mexico, it's a light bottled beer with a loyal following.
- *Corona* (koh ROH nah). The beer that crossed the border and became a status foreign beer in the United States is bottled as Corona Clara (KLA rah), a light beer.
- *Dos Equis* (dohs eh KEES). The name means two xx's and it's a popular dark beer.
- *Michelada* (mee cheh LAH dah) is beer with fresh lime squeezed into it and served in a salt-rimmed glass.
- *Moctezuma Sol Especial* (mock teh SOO mah sohl ehs peh see YAHL). Designed to compete head to head with Corona, a light beer.
- *Montejo* (mohn TEH hoh), *León Negro* (leh OHN NEH groh), and *Carta Clara* (KAR tah KLAH rah) are produced and sold in the Yucatán Peninsula. (See also *Michelada* and *Suero* below.)
- *Negra Modelo* (NEH grah moh DEH loh). A dark bottled beer distinguished from its sister *Modelo* (moh DEH loh), which is a light canned beer.

- *Noche Buena* (NOH cheh boo WEH nah). A dark beer produced for the Christmas season.
- *Superior* (soo PEH ree yohr). A light beer in tall brown bottles.
- *Tecate* (teh KAH teh). A canned beer (sometimes found in large bottles), traditionally imbibed with fresh lime and salt rubbed on the can or glass rim.
- *Tres Equis* (trehs eh KEES). The name means three xxx's and it's a canned lager beer.

Charanda (cha RAHN dah). A Michoacán aguardiente that's often served mixed with orange juice.

Ginebra (hee NEH brah). Gin.

Jerez (heh REHS). Sherry.

Lechugilla (leh choo GEEH yah). A maguey-like plant produces lechugilla, a mezcál-like home brew found in the Copper Canyon.

Mezcál (mehs KAHL). A distilled liquor. Made from another kind of agave (not the blue agave that produces tequila), it is the one with a worm (gusano) in the bottom of the bottle. The critter lives on the plant (until it meets an untimely end winding up in the bottom of the bottle or is collected for serving fried in restaurants), and is the signature by which you know you're buying true mezcál. Mezcál is most visible in Oaxaca where distilleries abound and sample glasses are proffered to tempt buyers. But drinking mezcál is also a tradition in Zacatecas at late-night street dancing and singing while following a mezcál-laden burro and a band, and in Guanajuato where estudiantinas singers lead the mezcál-bearing burro and the singing crowd through narrow sixteenth-century streets.

Michelada (mee cheh LAH dah). Beer with fresh lime added that's served in a salt-rimmed glass.

Pox (posh). Chiapa-style aguardiente that's served in hot fruit punch.

Rompope (rohm POH peh). An eggnog-like drink created by colonial-era nuns in Puebla, made with milk, sugar, vanilla, egg yolks, and rum. It's served at many festivities but especially around Christmas. Rompope is bottled commercially and makes a nice gift. (See also Market Buying Tips: *Rompope.*)

Ron (rohn). Rum. *Bacardi* (bah kahr DEE), or rum, is made in Mexico along with several other brands including Ron Potosí, an excellent brand from a small distillery near Ciudad Valles, Tamaulipas.

Sidra (SEE drah). Cider. Huejotzingo, a colonial-era town near Cholula and Puebla, southeast of Mexico City, is famous for local apple cider called the "champagne of Mexico" that's bottled and sold there. Copa de Oro brand is a bit bitter while Soamy and Gota Real brands are sweeter.

Suero (SWEH roh). Beer over ice served with a wedge of lime in a glass with a lime-wet rim that's been dipped in salt. (See also *Michelada* above.)

Tequila (teh KEE lah). Probably Mexico's best-known alcoholic beverage, tequila is distilled from the juicy heart of the blue agave (ah GAH veh) grown only in the Mexican states of Jalisco, Nayarit, and Michoacán. Its name comes from Tequila, Jalisco, the town around which the greatest quantity of blue agave is grown. The best tequila is 100 percent pure, without additives such as sugar. Excellent brands are Herradura, Patrón, El Tesoro de Don Felipe, and Chinaco.

Knowledge of this intriguing beverage has become so sophisticated that fine restaurants are beginning to present a tequila list in the way a wine list is offered. A tequilier (a person schooled in tequilas) may also be on hand to help with the selection, much the same as a wine steward.

However top-drawer it's becoming, tequila can betray the unwary. There is a saying about this national beverage: "Two tequilas you feel rich, four tequilas you feel good-looking, six tequilas you're bulletproof, and eight tequilas you're invisible." More than enough of this sly drink can make you think you speak and sing in Spanish fluently, even when the reverse is true.

Foreigners often think of tequila in relation to the frosty margarita, which is a mixed drink of tequila, triple sec or cointreau, and fresh lime juice served on the rocks or a frosty slush in a salt-rimmed glass.

(However, finding a good margarita in Mexico may require sipping some bitter brews in the process.) Mexicans, however, seldom mention a margarita and tequila in the same sentence, since they prefer to sip tequila plain from a shot glass paired with a shot glass of fresh lime, or with a spicy chaser such as *sangrita* (sahn GREE tah). The latter is a pleasantly spicy blend of tomatoes, orange juice, and ground dried chile.

Though party fun in Mexico may call for downing a shot glass of tequila in a couple of gulps alternated by licking lime juice and salt from the space between a closed thumb and index finger, Mexican tequila connoisseurs grimace at the unrefined practice. (Tourists who succumb to the shot-glass routine get a heady start on the evening after which there may be no memory of dueling tequila shots, or of how the bravado brought them to a view of the underside of the bar room table.)

- *Añejo* (ah NYEH hoh). Aged tequila. It spends at least a year in oak barrels.
- *Reposado* (reh poh SAH doh). Rested tequila. The smooth and refined or "rested" tequila is sipped slowly before a meal as you would a good brandy. It's golden color springs from the aging process in oak barrels, which lasts for at least two months or a year or more.
- *Tequila Blanco* (teh KEE lah BLAHN koh). White tequila that isn't aged. It's also called *tequila plata* (teh KEE lah PLAH tah) or silver tequila. It can

be joltingly strong or smooth enough for sipping as a fine cognac.

- *Tequila de Oro* (teh KEE lah deh OH roh). Gold tequila. It receives its color from artificial colorings or the addition of caramel.

Vino (BEEH noh). Wine. A glass of wine in Mexico is called a *copa de vino* (KOH pah deh BEE noh), translating literally to a "cup of wine." Dependable wines are Hidalgo Blanc de Blanc, Pedro Domec, and anything from the Casa Martell (a Mexican branch of the famed French company).

- *Vino Blanco* (BEEH noh BLAHN koh). White wine.
- *Vino Rojo* (BEEH noh ROH hoh). Red wine.
- *Vino Tinto* (BEEH noh TEEN toh). Rosé.

Wine was needed for Catholic Church rituals (not to mention for private consumption), so Mexico's grape industry got an early start with the blessing of the Spanish crown after the conquest of Mexico in the early 1500s. By 1595, however, King Phillip II of Spain prohibited the fledgling industry since it threatened to compete with wine making in Spain. Nevertheless, the grapes continued to be harvested albeit somewhat surreptitiously even though the plant failed to be a hearty performer. The first formally established wine producer was Francisco de Urdiñola, in the late sixteenth century at the Hacienda del Rosario, near Santa María de las Parras, Coahuila. Jesuit friar Junipero Serra introduced grape vines when he established the California missions. By the mid 1800s, twenty years after Mexico won independence from Spain in 1821, the industry began to thrive. Then the Mexican Revolution from 1910–17 caused a major setback. Only within the last twenty years has the industry begun to flourish. Today good wine is produced in Baja California, around Tequisquiapan in Querétaro state, Hidalgo, Chihuahua, Coahuila, Zacatecas, and Aguascalientes. Tequisquiapan, Querétaro, near the city of Querétaro, north of Mexico City, hosts a wine and cheese festival each May.

Liqueurs

Licores (lee KOH rehs). Liqueurs. A number of licores are worth seeking in Mexico. Here's a short list.

- *Damiana* (dah mee YAH nah). A liqueur made from the damiana plant. The plant is grown and sold throughout Mexico and is considered by Mexicans to be an aphrodisiac. As a drink it's taken after dinner—but it could appear in a margarita.
- *Kahlúa* (kah LOO ah). Coffee liqueur. Made with coffee, Kahlúa leads the pack in recognition and it's a welcome gift.
- *La Pasita* (lah pah SEE tah). For several decades La Pasita brand fruit liqueurs have been putting a blush on patrons' cheeks in Puebla. One of them, the *China Poblana* (CHEE nah poh BLAH nah), is three different liqueurs poured in three

levels—red, green, and white—representing the colors of the flag of Mexico. The *pasa* (PAH sah), or raisin, flavor is the most popular.

- *Xanath* (HAH nahth). A vanilla liqueur. It lines store shelves in the town of Papantla, in northern Veracruz state, which is in the heart of Mexico's vanilla-growing region.

- *Xtabentum* (ish tah ben TOOM). An anise-flavored Yucatecan fermented honey liqueur.

Fermented Drinks

Though most fermented drinks are worth trying, and the tuba is absolutely delicious, drinks sold by street vendors aren't made with trustworthy water. Try them in a good restaurant that assures the water source.

Pulque (POOL keh). A pre-Conquest beverage served to the ruling class, pulque is a pungent and lightly alcoholic beverage made from the fermented sap from yet another kind of agave—a different one from the tequila agave. According to folklore, pulque is good for diabetes. Flavoring with fresh fruit called *pulque curado* (POOL key kooh RAH doh) makes it more palatable to foreign tastes, though it's seldom served in tourist haunts except around Garibaldi Square in Mexico City. At small-town markets you may see men moving through the market with a pitcher and cup in hand heading to the local *pulqueria* (pool keh REE ah) hangout. They'll chat with the guys while sipping a few, then fill up the pitcher for takeout. Hidalgo is the Mexican state best known for pulque production, where it's also canned. But Mexicans abhor the canned version, preferring the frothy drink fresh from the fermenting process. The ancient god of pulque is honored at a mountaintop pyramid overlooking Tepoztlán, Morelos, southwest of Mexico City.

Tepache (teh PAH cheh). Fermented pineapple and brown sugar.

Tesquino/Tesguino/Teshuino/Tejuino (teh SKEE noh/teh GWEE noh/teh SWEE noh/teh WEE noh). Known by many names, it's a drink of freshly ground corn that's been fermented and to which brown sugar has been added. It's the central drink at Tarahumara Indian festivals in the state of Chihuahua, but the drink is sold in markets and by street vendors in other states as well.

Tuba (TOOH bah). A delicious drink made of fermented palm fiber and sugar mixed with water and often flavored with fruit. At serving it's sprinkled with ground nuts. In the states of Jalisco and Colima you'll often see young tuba sellers with a shoulder pole balancing two large natural gourds filled with the drink and capped with a dried corn cob. Buying from a colorful street vendor, however, is dangerous since it's impossible to know the source of the water.

COMFORT FOODS

· ■ ·

Although one joy of traveling in a foreign country is testing the local cuisine, there are times when travelers simply want something comfortable and familiar. This section provides the basics in English to find these comfort foods in Spanish.

English-Spanish

Bacon. *Tocino* (toh SEE noh).

Beans. *Frijoles* (free hoh lehs).

Beef. *Bif* (beef) or *res* (rehs). To tell the waiter how you'd like the meat cooked use these terms: *bien cocido* (bee YEHN koh SEE doh) is well done. It's the opposite of *poco cocido* (POH koh koh SEE doh) meaning rare. *Medio turno* (meh dee oh TOOR noh) means medium well done.

Beer. *Cerveza* (SEHR beh sah). (For the varieties see Beverages A to Z: *Cerveza.*)

Bread. *Pan* (pahn).

Butter. *Mantequilla* (mahn teh KEE yah).

Candy. *Dulces* (DOOL sehs).

Cereal. *Cereal* (SEH reh ahl). Kellogg's Corn Flakes and Raisin Bran are two cereals served by restaurants and breakfast buffets. Other U.S. brands are generally absent.

Cheez Whiz. *Cheez Whiz* (cheez wheez). The same brand sold in the United States is available in Mexico. (See also Market Buying Tips: *Cheez Whiz*.)

Chicken. *Pollo* (POH yoh). The simplest and most common rendition is grilled or pan-fried chicken in its skin, *pollo asado* (POH yoh ah SAH doh) or *pollo frito* (POH yoh FREE toh), usually accompanied by refried beans, rice, sometimes french fries, and lettuce topped with a couple of tomato slices and rings of freshly sliced white onion. Several excellent soups also include chicken as a main ingredient. Only at U.S.-style fast-food restaurants is chicken dipped in a batter and fried. (See also entries for *Caldo de Pollo* and *Sopa Tlalpeño* for soups of interest in the Menu Primer.)

Coffee. *Café* (kah FEH). (See *Café* entries in Market Buying Tips and Beverages A to Z: *Nonalcoholic Drinks.*)

Cookies. *Galletas* (gah YEH tahs). The word is the same as for crackers.

Corn. *Eloté* (eh LOH teh) or *maíz* (mah EEZ). Corn on the cob isn't served much in restaurants, but elote, as the cob kind is called, is available steaming hot from street vendors. Fresh corn kernels, however, figure in many vegetable soups and in corn soup. Maíz is used when talking about *masa de maíz* (MAH sah deh mah EEZ), the dough used for corn tortillas and tamales.

Crab. *Jaiba* (HI bah). The edible blue crab is predominant, but stone crab claws, *manitas de cangrejo* (mah NEE tahs deh kahn GREH hoh), are found primarily on the Yucatán Peninsula.

Crackers. *Galletas* (gah YEH tahs). Many brands of salad crackers are produced in Mexico. The word is the same for cookies.

Cream of Wheat. *Masa de harina* (MAH sah deh ah REE nah).

Doughnut. *Dona* (DOH nah). Dona is obviously a corruption of the English pronunciation, nevertheless signs reading DONAS proudly announce where doughnuts are sold. Even English speakers go along with the Mexican pronunciation. Mexicans make superb doughnuts in most varieties foreigners are accustomed to in their home countries.

Eggs. *Huevos* (WEH bohs). Besides the many ways Mexicans prepare eggs that are mentioned in the Menu Primer, plain scambled eggs or eggs with ham or bacon are available everywhere. (See also Market Buying Tips: *Huevos*.)

Fish. *Pescado* (pehs KAH doh). (See also *Seafood* below.)

- **Bass.** *Corvina* (kor BEE nah).
- **Black Bass.** *Lobino* (loh BEE noh).
- **Mahimahi.** *Dorado* (doh RAH doh).
- **Perch.** *Mojara* (moh HAH rah).

- **Salmon.** *Salmón* (sahl MOHN); *salmón ahumado* (sahl MOHN ah hooh MAH doh) is smoked salmon.
- **Sardines.** *Sardinas* (sahr DEE nahs).
- **Shad.** *Sábalo* (SAH bah loh).
- **Trout.** *Trucha* (TROO chah).
- **Tuna.** *Atún* (ah TOON).

French Fries. *Papas fritas* (PAH pahs FREE tahs). Large, thick, hand-sliced french fries are more the norm in Mexico rather than slender machine-made ones seen in the United States.

Green Beans. *Ejote* (eh HOH teh) or *habichuela* (hah bee chweh lah).

Hamburger. *Hamburguesa* (ahm boor GEH sah). Flavorful, close cousins to U.S.-style hamburgers are found almost everywhere in Mexico. However, juicy, flame-broiled meat is almost nonexistent, and the buns are less stout. Yellow cheese, mayonnaise, and ketchup all taste slightly different in Mexico and this influences the taste of the hamburger. The Mexican custom of adding a sliver of *jalapeño* chile can be a startling reminder of where you are.

Honey. *Miel* (mee YEHL).

Hot Dog. *Salchicha* (sahl CHEE chah). Also called hot dog as in English, or in Spanish *perro caliente* (PEH rroh kah lee YEHN teh), which is a literal translation of hot dog. Mayonnaise and mustard are usually offered, but sweet pickle relish is not customary. Usual condiments include a sprinkling of chile peppers, salsa cruda, and rich cream. Mexican hot dog buns are more flavorful than their American cousins.

Ice Cream. *Helado* (eh LAH doh). Venture into the pleasing variety of flavors of Mexican ice cream made from many flavors including mango, rum, rompope, raisins, and cajeta. (See also Menu Primer A to Z: *Helado*.)

Jam. *Mermilada* (mehr mee LAH dah).

Juice. *Jugo* (HOO goh). *Jugo de naranja* (HOO goh deh nah RAHN hah) is orange juice.

Ketchup. *Salsa catsup* (SAHL sah KAHT soop). Mexican ketchup is sweet and thin.

Lettuce. *Lechuga* (leh CHOO gah).

Mayonnaise. *Mayonesa* (meh oh NEH sah). Mexican mayonnaise has a slight hint of fresh lime, making it deliciously tangier than its American counterpart.

Milk. *Leche* (LEH cheh).

Mushroom. *Champiñón* (cham peen YOHN) or *hongo* (OHN goh) or *seta* (SEH tah).

Mustard. *Mustaza* (moohs TAH sah).

Oatmeal. *Avena* (ah BEH nah). This breakfast food is readily available in restaurants and grocery stores.

Onion. *Cebolla* (seh BOH yah). Onion soup, *sopa de cebolla* (SOH pah deh seh BOH yah), is generally very good in Mexico. The word may also be handy if you want onions for a taco, or to sprinkle on soup.

Pancake. *Pancake* or *hot cake*. In cities accustomed to tourists, waiters pronounce it the English way. But in villages where English is not widely spoken it may be pronounced "pahn KAH keh" or "hoht KAH keh." Maple syrup (MAH pleh), or more often local honey called *miel* (me YEHL), is the topping.

Pasta. *Pasta* (PAHS tah). Pronounced the same in English or Spanish, traditional Italian pasta finds its way to the menus of countless restauarants in Mexico. However, Mexican substitutes for oregano, bell peppers, basil, and Parmesan cheese and skimping on the garlic and tomato or meat sauce often mean the meal may be filling but somewhat lacking in Italian flavor. Pasta salads are a rarity.

Peanut Butter. *Crema de cacahuate* (KREH mah deh kah kah WAH teh).

Pepper. *Pimienta* (pee MEE yehn tah). Black pepper.

Pizza. *Pizza* (PEET sah). The pronunciation is the same in Mexico, but the taste varies. (See Menu Primer A to Z: *Pizza*.)

Potato. *Papa* (PAH pah). Fried is *frito* (FREE toh); french fries are *papas francés* (PAH pahs frahn SEHS); mashed potatoes are *puré* (poo REH); and baked potatoes are *al horno* (ahl OHR noh).

Rice. *Arroz* (ah ROHS). (See also Menu Primer A to Z: *Arroz*.)

Rum. *Ron* (rohn). (See also Beverages A to Z: *Alcoholic Drinks/Ron*.)

Salad. *Ensalada* (ehn sah LAH dah).

Salad Dressing. *Aderezo* (ah dah REHS oh).

Salt. *Sal* (sahl). Table salt.

Sandwich. *Torta* (TOHR tah). The word sandwich is also used and is generally understood even by

those who don't speak English. (See also Re-
gional/Seasonal Specialties: *Torta*.)

Sausage. You'll especially encounter three kinds:

- *Chorizo* (choh REE soh). A sausage with a strong
  reddish color and red chile flavor. It's offered with
  eggs and tacos.
- *Longaniza* (lohn gah NEE sah). A cured link
  sausage stuffed with pork, flavored with chiles
  and spices, and presented fried or in a green
  sauce.
- *Salchicha* (sahl CHEE chah). Hot dog or a German-
  style sausage.

Seafood. *Mariscos* (mah REES kohs).

Shrimp. *Camarón* (kah mah ROHN).

Soup. *Sopa* (SOH pah). Served both wet as a traditional soup, and dry as *sopa seca* (SOH pah SEH
kah), meaning a plate of rice. (See also Menu Primer
A to Z: *Sopa, Sopa Seca*, and *Caldo* and Regional/Sea-
sonal Specialties: *Sopa*.)

Sour Cream. *Crema agria* (KREH mah AH gree
yah). Only the most sophisticated restaurants catering to tourists serve tart sour cream as it's known in
the United States. Most Mexican cream used on food
(not coffee cream) is thick, incredibly rich, tasty, and
mildly sweet.

Spaghetti. Spelled spaghetti on menus, but the
Spanish spelling (which you seldom see) is *espageti*
(ehs pah GHEH tee) so waiters pronounce it as
though it begins with an "s."

Spaghetti Soup. *Sopa de fideo* (SOH pah deh fee DEH oh). Vermicelli floating in a tomato broth.

Steak. *Bifstek/Bistec* (beef stehk/BEE stehk). Beef served in ordinary Mexican restaurants is often tougher than most American beef but imported U.S. cuts are often featured in better establishments. Mexican beef quality, however, is improving rapidly, especially in the northern states of Sonora and Chihuahua, which supply some of the best steak houses in Mexico. Beef used in carne asado a la Tampiqueño is usually tender, but the cheaper cut used in milanesa (a breaded steak) may be pounded into delightful tenderness or left on its own and be, therefore, unchewable. Delicious stewed beef dishes such as carne guisada and tinga are reliably tender choices. (See also Menu Primer A to Z: *Bif.*)

Stone Crabs. *Manitas del Cangrejo* (mah NEE tahs del kohn GREH hoh).

Sugar. *Azucar* (ah SOO kahr).

Tangerine. *Mandarina* (mahn dah REE nah). Grown in Mexico and widely sold in open-air markets.

Tea. *Té* (teh). *Té negro* (teh NEH groh) or black tea is quite common. The tea recommended for sick stomachs is chamomile called *te de manzanilla* (teh deh mahn zah NEE yah). Iced tea is *té helado* (teh LAH doh).

Toast. *Pan Tostado* (pahn tohs TAH doh).

Tomato. *Tomate* (toh MAH teh). *Jitomate* (hee toh MAH teh) or *tomate roja* (toh MAH teh ROH hah) meaning red tomato. Not to be confused with *tomate verde* (toh MAH teh BEHR deh) meaning green tomato, which is not a tomato, but a firm, green, tomato-shaped fruit with a thin paper husk that's an ingredient in green chile salsa.

Turkey. *Pavo* (PAH boh).

V-8 Juice. *Jugo de Verduras* (HOOH goh deh behr DOO rahs).

Vinegar. *Vinagre* (bee NAH greh).

Wine. *Vino* (BEE noh). With Mexico's excellent wines, travelers don't lack for choice.

Worcestershire Sauce. *Salsa Inglesa* (SAHL sah een GLEH sah).

Yogurt (YOH goort). Yogurt. It's spelled a lot of ways in Mexico, all generally recognizable as yogurt. Flavored, commercially packaged yogurts aren't available but many restaurants are proud to offer fresh yogurt with honey, fruit, and granola. Almost all breakfast buffets have this combination.

REGIONAL/SEASONAL
SPECIALTIES

· ■ ·

THE SAME basic foods found throughout Mexico vary greatly in preparation from state to state and region to region. This section lists food first by name as it will appear on a menu. The names are then followed by the food variations by state or region and also by season.

Arroz (ah RROHS). Rice. Rice, the ubiquitous accompaniment to many Mexican meals, is served in a variety of ways throughout the country. (See also Menu Primer S to Z: *Arroz.*) Two special ones are as follows:

- *Arroz con mariscos* (ah RROHS kohn mah REEZ kohs). Rice with seafood served in Campeche, a Gulf Coast fortified city on the Yucatán Peninsula. White rice is often embellished with shrimp, crab, and oysters and served as an accompaniment to a main course.
- *Arroz poblano* (ah RROHS poh BLAH noh).

Puebla-style rice. Corn kernels, mixed with bits of poblano pepper, join white rice for a dish that's found in the state of Puebla. (See also Menu Primer A to Z: *Arroz*.)

Barbacoa (bahr bah KOH ah). Barbecue. Though nothing like barbecue in the United States, Mexico's regional variations are worth trying wherever you are. In particular Zacatecas, towns around the ruins of Teotihuacán near Mexico City, and the state of Mexico are well known for their barbecue. Jalisco state takes pride in its borrego (lamb roasted on a spit). In Tlaxcala, cooks use fish or wild game, and add sliced nopal cactus to their version of a barbecue sauce that's cooked in mixiote (maguey parchment paper) wrappers and called barbacoa en mixiote. (See also *Mixiotes* below and Menu Primer A to Z: *Barbacoa*.)

Birria (BEE rree yah). Lamb, goat, pork, or veal baked and served in a mild red sauce. A specialty of Jalisco state, it floats in enough flavorful thin liquid to make it look like a soup—but it isn't called soup. When there's no special notice announcing birria, it's usually listed under meat on the menu. However, most places that serve it serve only birria. The adeptly seasoned sauce includes chiles, cloves, onion, cumin, tomatoes, cloves, oregano, and pepper, but it isn't picante. To eat it, cut the meat in bite-size pieces, put them in a tortilla with chopped onions and cilantro, then dip it in the sauce and *carumba*! What a dish! (See also Menu Primer A to Z: *Birria*.)

Borrego (bohr REH goh). Lamb. In the state of Jalisco flayed and seasoned lamb roasts over an open wood fire at countryside restaurants and especially in the village of Tapalpa. In Zacatecas, borrego is marinated in an adobo sauce and then baked in an oven. In Puebla state, *mixiotes* (mee SHOH tehs), which are pieces of lamb marinated in a chile sauce and steamed in a parchment paper, make one of the most delicious ways to feast on lamb.

Botana (boh TAH nah). Appetizers or antojitos. Many of the fried masa (cornmeal-based) botanas mentioned below are essentially the same thing but with different names, depending on the region or state.

- *Bocoles* (boh KOH lehs). From the state of San Luis Potosí come tasty treats made of fried masa that's stuffed with sausage, cheese, and chorizo.
- *Chalupa* (cha LOO pah). A canoe-shaped masa appetizer that's the same as a tlacoyo. (See also *Botana/Tlacoyo* below and Menu Primer A to Z: *Chalupa*.)
- *Garnacha* (gahr NAH chah). The Yucatán Peninsula gives us a thick small cake of fried corn masa dough formed into a circle with the sides pinched to hold the toppings. The toppings include a thin layer of refried black beans and tomato sauce and tart crumbled cheese.
- *Gorditas* (gohr DEE tahs). It's impossible to list all the foods with this name in Mexico, but to give an indication of its variety a few are listed here.

In Tamaulipas masa cakes, called gorditas, are deep-fried to a nearly crispy golden brown in lard and served with black beans, avocado or guacamole, and red salsa. On Sundays around the Parque Morelos in San Luis Potosí, street vendors stuff fried masa patties with pureed beans, cheese, chile strips, ground meat or pork skin, and salsa. Something made like a panucho (see below) is also called a gordita in some locales. (See also Botana/Itacate below.)

- *Itacate* (ee tah KAH teh). In Hidalgo state cooks make a thick patty (gordita) of corn masa mixed with cow bone marrow, which is fried and bathed in a green chile sauce. The word itacate usually means take-home food (as in leftovers from a meal that a hostess might offer).

- *Memelas* (meh MEH lahs). Served in Oaxaca and Morelos, these meal starters begin like so many others with a fried cornmeal masa base. Topped with a tomato sauce that's seasoned with serrano chiles, the whole is sprinkled with cheese.

- *Panuchos* (pah NOO chohs). A Yucatán specialty in which corn tortillas are cut to create a thin pocket that is stuffed with refried beans and an egg slice and then fried to a crisp. Another version calls for the ingredients (turkey and onions) to garnish the top. Though served all over the Yucatán Peninsula, two villages near Mérida, Kansín and Umán, are so well known for them that the places where they are served are called *panucherías* (pah noo cheh REE ahs).

- *Picada* (pee KAH dah). The Veracruz cousin of the *sope* (see below) is the picada. However, a picada in Puebla is quite another morsel. There, it's prepared more like an enchilada without a filling. A small corn tortilla is fried in lard and covered with chopped white onion and either a red or green sauce.

- *Sope* (SOH peh). The sope, yet another appetizer that begins with a fried cornmeal base, complicates the botana issue. Similar to the garnacha, the sope, which is called by that name more in central Mexico, is round and may be a bit more heaped than a garnacha. Shredded chicken or crumbled sausage may be added. Pickled red onions may sit in for the chopped white ones and a green sauce may substitute for the red sauce.

- *Tlacoyo/Tlatloyo* (tlah KOH yoh/tlaht LOH yoh). The botana of this name is found more often in central Mexico than elsewhere, particularly in small local restaurants and markets, and when sold by street vendors. The masa is shaped into an oval resembling the form of a canoe and mashed beans are spread on the bottom; then it's topped with salsa, onions, and cheese or sour cream and fried. It's the same as a chalupa mentioned above.

- *Totopo* (toh TOH poh). In Michoacán a totopo is corn tortilla dough mixed with beans, flattened, and deep-fried for an edible platter hidden under a mound of guacamole or spicy meat and onions. A totopo in Oaxaca, however, is a thick hard tortilla punched with holes. (See also Menu Primer A to Z: *Antojitos*.)

Cabrito (kah BREE toh). Roast kid goat. Northern Mexico, the domain of restaurants specializing in roasted infant goats, proffers a dismaying (to an outsider) assortment of parts of the goat to choose from—most of which appear on the menu without explanation. Locals, of course, know each part of the goat and tackle the menu easily. The rest of us need a graduate course in goat anatomy.

This may sound silly since we're talking about goats, but a properly cooked goat shouldn't smell goaty and shouldn't be greasy. However, be forewarned that tough, goaty-smelling, greasy cabrito is frequently served. Well-prepared cabrito should be fork-tender and so delicious that it's entered in your list of meals to repeat—that is the meaty parts—you may prefer to forget the "exotic" parts.

- *Cabecita* (kah beh SEE tah). With this we enter deep into goat territory: plain and simple cabecita is "little goat head." Aficionados of cabrito consider it a delicacy. The platter appears with a deep-fried goat head split open forming a heart shape on the plate with the inside up. It's served with flour tortillas, guacamole, salsa, and charro beans. The diner scoops out the brains and eyes into a tortilla, adds a dab of guacamole and salsa on top, rolls it up and chows down. There's enough for at least four or five tacos like that.

Now for the next step: Turn the goat over and try not to see that the critter has a big toothy smile. Begin pulling the crispy skin off the head and fill another tortilla, or just eat it straight—if you can.

- *Fritada* (free TAH dah). Literally, fried goat meat served in the animal's blood, or the blood fried into a patty shape.
- *Machito* (mah CHEE toh). The heart, kidneys, and liver wrapped in the stomach pouch.
- *Mollecas* (moh YEH kahs). The salivary glands.
- *Paleta* (pah LEH tah). Ordering this will summon the ribs and a leg.
- *Pecho* (PEH choh). This selection will bring ribs, leg, and outer stomach.
- *Pierna* (pee YEHR nah). Leg meat. Pierna offers the most meat without a struggle.
- *Renonda* (reh NOHN dah). Ribs and kidneys.

Caldo Michi (KAHL doh MEE chee). Catfish soup. Several states, including Guanajuato and Jalisco boast caldo michi as a specialty. The Lake Chapala region, south of Guadalajara, Jalisco, is especially well known for this caldo. In Guanajuato loads of vegetables embolden this popular bowlful. Table garnishes include chopped onions, chiles, oregano, and fresh lime. (See also *Sopa* below and Menu Primer A to Z: *Caldo*.)

Capeado (kah pee YAH doh). Vegetables fried with cheese. In Chiapas fresh green beans or chayote are sandwiched around a slice of Chihuahua cheese, dipped in a frothy egg-white batter, and fried.

Cazón (kah SOHN). Shark. Shark meat is seen more on menus in Campeche than elsewhere.

- *Bollos de Masa* (BOH yohs deh MAH sah). Another Campeche shark specialty. Round balls of masa are stuffed with ground shark that's been flavored with spices, then wrapped in corn or banana leaves and steamed—making something like a round tamal.
- *Pan de Cazón* (pahn deh kah SOHN). Shredded shark cooked in a sauce is served between two tortillas and eaten with a fork. It may be one of those acquired-taste dishes.
- *Tinquinipaal* (teen keen ee PAHL). A spicy pâté made of ground shark meat mixed with spices and chiles and served as a botana.

Cecina (seh SEE nah). Thin steak of salted pork. A specialty of Morelos state, the fame of cecina from Yecapixtla, a sixteenth-century village, east of Cuerna-vaca, is countrywide. Traditionally it's served with rich heavy cream and strips of grilled chile poblano, both of which cut the salty taste of the meat. (See also *Tasajo*.)

Cemitas (seh MEE tahs). A Puebla and Tlaxcala sandwich specialty. Restaurants in both states proudly announce cemitas, and some of them sell nothing else. The slightly spinning-top-shaped buns glittered with sesame seeds that are used for the sandwiches are called cemitas. Fillings range from three to ten choices including milanesa and shredded chicken, garnished with lettuce, tomatoes, onions, and sliced chile.

Ceviche (seh BEE cheh). Raw fish or seafood marinated in fresh lime juice. Bits of fresh seafood are marinated in lime juice along with serrano chiles, tomatoes, onion, cilantro, and olive oil. In Acapulco it's combined with a tangy tomato sauce (sometimes a bit like ketchup) in a large goblet and eaten with a fork accompanied by saltine crackers. Elsewhere the marinated fish or seafood is piled on a plate and eaten with tostadas (tohs TAH dahs), which are smallish fried or baked tortillas. Carrots are added to the mixture in Manzanillo, where it's a popular botana served free with drinks at the city's local drinking/snacking establishments called *bota-neros* (boh tah NEH rohs). Veracruz cooks top the mixture with slices of avocado, olives, and lime.

Chalupa (chah LOO pah). It's fried masa (a fine cornmeal) or tortillas with many regional variations. In Puebla, a corn tortilla is fried crisp, then topped with a red sauce, a sprinkling of cheese, a bit of shredded pork, chicken, or beef, and chopped onion. In other places it may be more like a fully loaded tostada. (See Menu Primer A to Z: *Chalupa* and *Tostada*.)

Chanclas (CHAN klahs). A specialty of Puebla, this bright red, sauce-covered sandwich is eaten with a fork. Because it's far more than a sandwich, chanclas are usually listed under menu entrees rather than in the list headed torta or sandwich. The filling consists of a special kind of delicious regional sausage that's fried and arranged on the bottom side of a large savory bun along with fresh slices of avocado and white onion. Then the top of the bun is added and it's all covered in the same peppy sauce used for mixiotes except that it's a thicker sauce.

Changleta (chan GLEH tah). A delicious stuffed chayote (squash) served in Chiapas as a dessert. Boiled chayote is scooped from its husk or shell, then baked with a mixture of milk, vanilla, and butter, all topped with raisins and bread crumbs.

Charales (chah RAH lehs). A small dried silvery fish resembling a minnow. Around Lake Pátzcuaro and Lake Chapala, where they are harvested, they are sold by the bagful for munching with beer, or for use in tacos. In Veracruz two different dishes combine charales with eggs and nopal (prickly pear) cactus.

Chiles en Nogada (CHEE lehs EN oh GAH dah). Considered the national dish of Mexico, it's a combination of green chiles poblano stuffed with sweetened meat, draped in a white walnut sauce, and sprinkled with brilliant red pomegranate seeds—

green, white, and red—the colors of the Mexican flag. This festive dish was created by Puebla nuns for the August 28 saint's day (St. Augustín) of Mexican emperor Augustín de Iturbide (who reigned briefly in the nineteenth century before being shot by a firing squad). Since then, owing to the colors, it's become an Independence Day (September 16) specialty, though it's served in both August and September when pomegranates are in season. The ingenious pepper stuffing has ground veal and pork fraternizing with onions, garlic, tomatoes, jalapeños, fresh pineapple, bananas, raisin, pears, fresh cinnamon, cloves, and almonds for a truly tantalizing taste. None of the ingredients are overwhelming, but it's pleasantly sweet and served chilled or warm. Restaurants often slap a special, temporary sign outside to announce this much-relished seasonal dish. Sample them everywhere, since no two cooks create the same flavor.

Chiles Rellenos (CHEE lehs reh YEH nohs). Stuffed chiles. Stuffed poblano peppers are usually meat- or cheese-filled, but where seafood is fresh, especially the Pacific Coast and Baja California, the stuffing may be seafood or mariscos (mah REES kohs) as the menu will read. It may be simply a filling of shrimp, which alone will be delicious, or it may combine shrimp or lobster with fish. Both will be seasoned with garlic, onion, tomatoes, and perhaps a hint of oregano. A red sauce is the usual topping but in Baja

California it could be a surprise béchamel sauce, which is a smooth French white sauce.

Chilmole (cheel MOH leh). A blackened pepper sauce used primarily in relleno negro, a specialty of the Yucatán Peninsula. Though the chile is cooked until it looks burned, the resulting sauce goes down without a hint of burned flavor. The paste from which the sauce is made is also called *relleno negro* (reh YEH noh NEH groh), *recado negro* (reh KAH doh NEH groh), and *chirmole* (cheer MOH leh). (See also *Chilmole* entries in Menu Primer A to Z and Market Buying Tips.)

Chilpachole (cheel pah CHOH leh). A Veracruz sauce used to stew meat and seafood. It's made with garlic, onion, tomatoes, and fiery chipotle chiles.

Chocolate (choh koh LAH teh). Chocolate. Though trees growing the large cacao (chocolate) bean are cultivated on plantations near Villahermosa in the state of Tabasco, and used throughout the country in the hundreds of varieties of mole sauce, prepared chocolate cakes are most widely sold in Oaxaca. There the rich aroma of fresh chocolate mixed with almonds, sugar, and cinnamon wafts from specialty stores that mix it according to the patron's specifications. Street vendors sell it in packages of thick, fifty-cent-size cakes. Besides Tabasco (where you can tour the plantations), and Oaxaca, cacao is also cultivated in Campeche, Chiapas, Veracruz, and

Guerrero. The beans are enclosed in huge football-sized pods that grow directly from the trunk and branches of the cacao tree. The beans are dumped from the large pod, fermented, then dried (becoming bitter) in preparation for mixture with sugar and other ingredients that make a palatable taste. In chocolate-growing regions many private plantation owners sell hard cakes of homemade chocolate to the public. At these private plantations visitors may be treated to a refreshing and unusual drink made by straining the outer fuzzy portion of fresh beans and mixing them with sugar. (See also *Chocolate* entries in Menu Primer A to Z and Market Buying Tips.)

Clemole (cleh MOH leh). A specialty stew of Taxco, Mexico's "Silver Capital." Between haunting the more than 200 shops selling silver in this town, you may have to sleuth the below-ground-level market stalls for clemole, but it's worth a hunt especially if the stew has had plenty of time to simmer and the meat is tender. On restaurant menus it would be listed under meat, but it's more like a caldo or soup. The basic, thin, and mildly fiery sauce balances ground pasilla chiles, chicken broth, onions, and garlic, while simmering green beans, large pieces of carrot, potato, corn on the cob, and large hunks of stew meat. Each serving holds a little of each ingredient with lots of the liquid, and arrives apportioned with corn tortillas, chopped onion, sliced serrano, and lime wedges.

Dulces (DOOHL sehs). Sweets, candy, or cookies. Startlingly sweet candied fruits and vegetables lead the lineup of Mexico's sweets and come wrapped for gift giving or for nibbling bit by bit. A concentrated dulce quest would include the ates and other sweets in the Mercado de Dulces in Morelia, northwest of Mexico City, and in the dulces section of the Mercado Merced in Mexico City, sweet shops in San Cristóbal de las Casas, in southern Mexico, special cookies and candy in Puebla, east of Mexico City, milk candy in San Juan de los Lagos, and the portales (arcades) in Toluca, west of Mexico City, especially around the Days of the Dead. (See *Dulce/Dulces* entries in Market Buying Tips and Menu Primer A to Z.)

Enchiladas (en chee LAH dahs). In most places an enchilada is a corn tortilla dunked in a red sauce and filled with meat or cheese and topped in a variety of ways. However, in Morelia, Pátzcuaro, and Oaxaca enchiladas may be no more than tortillas dunked in a red sauce, fried in oil, sprinkled with cheese and onions, and served three to an order—without a center filling. Pachuca-style enchiladas call for the tortillas to first be fried in lard, then dredged in a poblano chile sauce, then rolled up with a stuffing of shredded chicken or cheese, and crowned with sliced radish and lettuce. In San Luis Potosí, enchiladas may be deep-fried flautas (FLOUT ahs), but they may also be more traditionally prepared with chicken stuffing and topped with beans, avocado, cheese, and onion.

- *Enchiladas de leche* (en chee LAH dahs deh LEH cheh). In Durango state tortillas are moistened in a mixture of toasted chiles and milk, then fried and topped with chopped hard-boiled eggs.
- *Enchiladas mineras* (en chee LAH dahs mee NEH rahs). In Guanajuato, a colonial-era silver mining town in central Mexico, miner's enchiladas were meant to appease the appetites of hardworking miners. So the typical enchilada is flanked by fried chicken, carrots, and boiled potatoes, the latter three a reminder of the English who once ran the mines.
- *Enchiladas rojas* (en chee LAH dahs ROH hahs). In Aguascalientes, sausage, vegetables, and cheese are stuffed in flour tortillas to make the locally favored enchilada. It's then covered with sliced sausage and vegetables, and a sprinkling of chiles and cheese.

Ensalada de Noche Buena (en sah LAH dah deh NOH cheh BWHEN nah). Christmas Eve salad. This colorful and delicious salad combines beets, oranges, bananas, pineapple, jícama, peanuts, sugar, and vinegar or mayonnaise. It's sprinkled on top with shredded coconut and the whole concoction turns beet red for a perfect accompaniment to a festive meal.

Lonche (LOHN cheh). A Jalisco specialty sandwich in a long bun. In Guadalajara and throughout the state a long bun, with most of the bread scooped out of the middle, is then filled with a choice of meats, cheeses, avocado, tomato, and mayonnaise or cream and called a lonche.

Memelas (meh MEH lahs). An Oaxaca botana. (See also *Botana* above.)

Menudo (meh NOOH doh). Tripe stew. Featured especially on Saturday morning menus, as a hangover remedy, it's a rather intestinal-smelling chile and tomato broth brew that may take some getting use to. However, León, Guanajuato, serves menudo with an inviting twist. To the usual red broth base are added orange juice, red wine, almonds, oregano, olives, and raisins. Temporary signs announcing pancita (pahn SEE tah) may also mean menudo is being served, especially in and around Oaxaca and Mexico City. There, the word pancita (meaning little stomach) is used instead of menudo. (See also Menu Primer A to Z: *Menudo*.)

Mixiotes (mee SHOH tehs). Meat wrapped in parchment paper and steamed in a rich broth.

This delightful dish is especially popular in the states of Puebla, Hidalgo, and Tlaxcala and around the pyramids of Teotihuacán in the state of Mexico. Although there are special plastic bags sold just for steaming mixiotes on the stove top, traditionally a thin parchment paper made from the maguey plant becomes the "bag" to contain the ingredients during cooking.

The meat, which is either lamb, chicken, or rabbit, is chopped in larger than bite-sized pieces, marinated in a sauce, and tied up in the parchment paper bags, then steamed in a pit of hot coals in the ground or more conveniently on the stove.

In Puebla the meat is cooked and served in a marinade made of chile ancho, chile guajillo, garlic, cumin, oregano, and water. The cooked sauce should be very mild to the taste and not at all overpowering. If it tastes too strongly of the chile, then it's not a good sauce. The Tlaxcala version builds on the Puebla brew by adding black pepper, salt, cinnamon, onion, toasted avocado leaf, almonds, water or chicken broth, and vinegar. These are then oven-steamed. Teotihuacán mixiotes are more like a chicken or rabbit stew combined with carrots, onions, and potatoes. Cooks in Hidalgo (a state north of Mexico City) use a large variety of meats in their mixiotes, including pork, venison, and fish. They may also use nopal cactus leaves for flavor.

Traditionally served with a mild green sauce, sliced avocado, and tortillas, there's a particular way to eat mixiotes. First untie the string at the top of the bag, dribble the sauce across the contents inside the bag, cut the meat into bite sizes, put a portion of the meat into the soft tortilla with a slice of avocado, roll the tortilla to hold the contents, and begin the feast. (See also *Borrego* and *Barbacoa* above.)

Mole (MOH leh). Nearly every state honors this most Mexican of sauces with one or more renditions. Four or more different kinds of chiles are typically used, and the colors and varieties of chiles (along with the other twenty to thirty disparate ingredients) influence the taste from region to region. Oaxaca boasts seven moles, and may have cornered the Mexican mole market, although the sauce originated in Puebla state. The green and red pipiáns, which feature huge amounts of ground sesame seeds as a flavorful thickener, are also considered moles. A grand-sized mole festival, complete with competing cooks, is held each year sometime during the first three weeks of October in the village of San Pedro Actópan near Milpa Alta south of Mexico City. (Besides the moles highlighted below, see also *Pipián* below, Menu Primer A to Z: *Mole* and *Estofado*, and Market Buying Tips: *Mole*.)

- *Coloradito* (koh loh rah DEE toh). A Oaxaca mole, the tempting marriage of ingredients includes chiles, sesame seeds, almonds, raisins, bananas, and a variety of spices all of which are ladled over chicken.
- *Manchamanteles* (mahn chah mahn TEH lehs). Tablecloth stainer is the translation of this mole that's yellow/orange in color. The exotic blend features chiles, garlic, vinegar, onions, tomato, sausage, apples, pears, pineapple, and banana. The result is a whisper of picante mingled in the barely sweet flavor. No one region can claim it, since it's served so widely, although menus in Mexico City, and Puebla seem to feature it more often.

- *Mole Estilo Tlayacapan* (MOH leh ehs TEE loh tlah yah KAH pan). Tlayacapan, Morelos-style mole. Another of the sweet/picante moles, it mingles apples, bananas, and raisins in a mixture that also includes about equal parts chile pasilla and ground sesame seeds.
- *Mole negro* (MOH leh NEH groh). Black mole. Oaxaca is best known for a black mole that can be a bit bitter.
- *Mole de olla* (MOH leh deh OH yah). Pot-made mole. A specialty of Morelos, this mole includes cactus fruit and epazote (a pungent herb) cooked with pork, lamb, or cecina.
- *Mole poblano* (MOH leh poh BLAH noh). Puebla-style mole. Reddish-brown in color and sweeter than Oaxaca mole negro, mole poblano refers only to the mole from the city of Puebla. If you venture into the rest of that state, the moles will be different.
- *Mole de Xico* (MOH leh deh HEE koh). Mole from Xico, Veracruz. This town near Jalapa, Veracruz, offers some of the most delicious, faintly sweet, mole in the country.

Molotes (moh LOH tehs). A type of quesadilla. Typical quesadillas are formed using a flour tortilla folded (clam-shaped) over a filling of cheese or meat and then fried. Molotes, however, are shaped completely differently than a typical quesadilla, and the thin masa dough they're made with bubbles when fried, making a crispy wrapper.

- Around Papantla, in northern Veracruz state, deep-fried molotes are small (thumb-length), football-shaped morsels filled with cheese, potatoes, or meat.
- In Oaxaca City, the shape and filling are similar, but the molotes are a bit larger. These are often served in a lettuce leaf and topped with black bean paste.
- Puebla offers the King Kong of molotes. The fine thin masa is rolled out larger than a tortilla, then the filling of meat, cheese, and cooked poblano chile or mashed potato is spread over the center, after which it's rolled into a long open-at-the-top cone (like a rolled-up sheet of paper) and fried. The scrolling of the tortilla produces a molote that's eight or more inches long; it's presented standing in a glass or bowl and served with fresh green or red salsas for dipping and sometimes a garnish of chopped white onion and avocado. But Puebla-style molotes stand alone in taste without any added dips or garnish.

Monguls (mohn GOOLS). Marinated and baked pork rind. Usually seen as street vendor fare after it's deep-fried, in Hidalgo, chicharrón (pork rind) is prepared in an unusual dish called mongul. The pork rind is marinated in onion, garlic, vinegar, and other spices, then fried, wrapped in maguey leaves and baked. (See also Menu Primer A to Z: *Chicharrón.*)

Pambazo (pahm BAH soh). A sandwich. More often seen in and around Mexico City, the name of this warm sandwich comes from the name of the bun—pambazo. It's as large as a big man's hand, with two creases down the center. For the sandwich, it's sliced open, both sides are dipped in a thin red sauce, then fried to warming. While it's frying, the filling is added to one side—a slice or two of avocado, a few freshly sliced rings of onion, then chicken or sausage, sometimes potatoes and beans. It's wrapped in a napkin and ready for eating out of hand.

Pan (pahn). Bread. Discovering Mexico's hundreds of breads is a gastronomic adventure.

Tlaxcala is the state with the most visible bread. Whole villages there are devoted to making festival breads which are prepared for almost every special event in the country. They appear in a variety of shapes including tufted rounds, braided and long flatish loaves, all speckled with sesame seeds or some swirly design on top. Some are called yolk bread, which in Spanish is *pan de yema* (pahn deh YEH mah), and others are made without yolks. Some are sweetish and others savory. Baked by the dozens in room-sized brick ovens, Tlaxcala bread is then packed into crates, the design of which dates from pre-Hispanic times. Layers of moist leaves from a special tree keep the bread fresh to last through festivals hundreds of miles away. In Oaxaca City, the quantity and variety of breads displayed in the Mercado Abastos are truly astounding. Enormous piles of bread display puffy brioche-like round loaves, flat unleavened loaves, yolk bread, and much more.

Some of the specific regional breads by name include:

- *Cemita* (seh MEE tah). A special large, puffy delicious sandwich bun, sprinkled with sesame seeds, that's sold in Puebla. The same bun in Tlaxcala is spelled semita.
- *Pambazo* (pahm BAH soh). These buns, also for sandwiches, are large, flatish, and rather elongated with two creases in the middle. They are used to make fried sandwiches—but the soft, yeasty buns are delicious without frying. These are seen primarily in and around Mexico City.
- *Pan de Muerto* (pan deh MWEHR toh). Also called Days of the Dead Bread, this is sold all over the country for weeks before the actual Days of the Dead which are November 1–2. They come in a variety of forms—round loaves with mock bone-shaped bread draped across the top, others sculpted as plump human figures, and in round loaves with sugar faces adorning the outside. Some are frosted with colored or plain sugar, or have colored bread flowers, and other designs are baked in. Many are plain or scored decoratively before baking. Days of the Dead bread is eventually eaten, but the first use may be on an elaborate home altar dedicated in memory of deceased loved ones. These altars will also include samples of local foods, flowers, fruits, drinks, and memorabilia of the departed. But some altars are so large that a dozen or more loaves of bread are needed to balance the altar design.

Days of the Dead bread shows creative genius, or is provided in astounding abundance especially in Mexico City, Oaxaca, Toluca, and Valle de Bravo.

- *Pan de pulque* (deh POOL keh). Bakery shop signs emblazoned with PAN DE PULQUE dot the streets of Saltillo in northern Mexico. This specialty bread, made with pulque, the fermented juice of a special agave, comes in many flavors and shapes—all worth trying.

Pancita (pahn SEE tah). The name for menudo in and around Mexico City. (See also *Menudo* above and Menu Primer A to Z: *Menudo*.)

Pastes (PAHS tehs). English meat turnovers. English miners brought their pasties to the region around Pachuca and Real del Monte in the state of Hidalgo, northeast of Mexico City. Though a scaled-down version of this meal in a pastry pocket may be served today, the original was a large wheat flour pastry filled with a dense concoction of chicken, potatoes, carrots, and onions. Miners carried it flat against the stomach to keep it warm until lunch, which they often ate inside the mine. Among variations served today in this region are fillings of beef and beans.

Pavo (PAH boh). Turkey. In the Yucatán, cooks make special use of this versatile bird.

- *Pavo en Escabeche de Valladolid* (PAH boh en ehs kah BEH cheh deh bah yah doh LEED). Originating in Valladolid, Yucatán, it's turkey in a pickle sauce that's served far beyond town borders. Tangy, not wildly pickled in taste, the dish comes together when a turkey breast or leg is covered in a clear broth flavored with bay leaves and rings of pickled red onions, and sometimes accompanied by bowls of green and red salsa for added flavor.

• *Pavo en Relleno Blanco* (PAH boh en reh YEH noh BLAHN koh). Another Yucatecan specialty, it features chunks of turkey breast covered in a white sauce made with wheat flour and flavored with onions, capers, almonds, and raisins. A dribble of bright red tomato sauce makes for a colorful dish, although it can be rather bland to the taste. Ask for a side order of rice to absorb the extra sauce.

• *Pavo en Relleno Negro* (PAH boh en reh YEH noh NEH groh). This Yucatecan dish offers a delicious stuffing for turkey. A turkey leg or breast is the meat of choice that's stuffed with a mixture of onions, garlic, pork, banana, apples, raisins, and almonds. That's the traditional preparation, but don't be surprised if what passes for the dish are slices of turkey breast in a black sauce. The thin and lightly picante black sauce that covers it is made with blackened chiles, chicken stock, onions, tomato, and wine. The sauce is called relleno negro, chirmole, chilmole, or recado negro. (For more on relleno negro, see *Chilmole* entries in Menu Primer A to Z and Market Buying Tips.)

Pellizcada (peh YEES KAH dah). A Veracruz-style tortilla. (See also *Tortilla/Pellizcada* below.)

Pescado a la Talla (pehs KAH doh ah lah TAH yah). Red snapper grilled with a delicious a la Talla seasoning and a specialty of Acapulco. The mixture of ground spices that's rubbed on the butterflied fish before cooking includes ancho and morita chiles, garlic, onion, oregano, cumin, a bit of cinnamon, vinegar, and mayonnaise.

Pipián (pee pee YAHN). A green or red sauce thickened with roasted and ground squash, sesame, and melon seeds. Pipiáns are considered moles. (Besides the following, see also *Mole* above and Market Buying Tips: *Pipián*.)

- *Pipián Rojo* (pee pee YAHN ROH hoh). The red version may feature ground seeds of achiote, or it may get its redness from tomatoes and ground dried chiles. Pipián rojo is found more on menus in the Yucatán Peninsula and Puebla.
- *Pipián Verde* (pee pee YAHN BEHR deh). Green pipián. Green sauce ingredients vary, but the basic form mingles ground melon seeds, green chiles, peanuts, and tomate verde, all ground together and cooked in a chicken broth. Swiss chard, spinach, and hoja santa (an anise-flavored leaf) may also be used. Pipián verde is found more in central Mexico, especially Puebla. Puebla cooks serve pipián verde over chunky pieces of pork loin.

Poc Chuc (pohk CHOOK). Marinated grilled pork. Invented in the Mérida, Yucatán, kitchen of El Restaurante Los Almendros, this dish swept the peninsula, rapidly becoming a regional specialty. The taste will be different each time you have it depending on the cook's hand in the marinade, which features sour orange juice, tomato, onion, garlic, and chiles.

Pollo (POH yoh). Chicken. Chicken, a prominent fixture in Mexico's cuisine, appears in many innovative ways.

- *Pollo del Jardín de San Marcos* (POH yoh dehl har DEEN deh sahn MAR kohs). Chicken sold around the plaza called Jardín (garden) San Marcos. This is a specialty of Aguascalientes, which hosts the annual San Marcos Fair during April and May. Chicken, fried sausage, and potatoes share the engaging sauce made of tomatoes and chicken broth sprinkled with onions, vinegar, and other spices.
- *Pollo pibil* (POH yoh pee BEEL). Pit-baked chicken is one of the most pleasing specialties of the Yucatán Peninsula. The chicken is covered in achiote preparado, tomatoes, and onions, wrapped in banana leaves and baked in an earthen pit called a *pib* (peeb). Like its cousin *cochinita pibil* (koh chee NEE tah pee BEEL), which is made with pork, this mild but delicious specialty is almost always a pleasingly tasty dish to order.

- *Pollo a la plaza* (POH yoh ah lah PLAH sah). Plaza chicken. A comforting platterful of food, plaza chicken was once served only by street vendors around plazas in Pátzcuaro and Morelia, Michoacán. Now it's a restaurant specialty as well. Pollo is fried with large slices of potatoes, carrots, and onions. The traditional accompaniment with this already filling meal are *enchiladas enfrijoladas* (en chee LAH dahs en free hoh LAH dahs).
- *Pollo Ticuleño* (POH yoh tee koo LEN yoh). Originating in Ticul, Yucatán, this scrumptious, layered platterful is now found on menus throughout the peninsula. From the bottom up it begins with a large circle of smooth tomato sauce, then a thick round of mashed potatoes or cooked ground masa (corn dough), followed by a crispy baked corn tortilla, on top of which is placed the breaded chicken breast. It comes piping hot and dappled with shredded cheese and green peas.

Pozole (poh SOH leh). A filling hominy and pork or chicken soup of pre-Hispanic origin. Pozole is such a popular soup that you'll see temporary signs posted at restaurants announcing HAY POZOLE, meaning "There's pozole today." Table condiments typically served in little bowls are oregano, chopped white onions, sliced radish, and shredded cabbage or lettuce. From each condiment bowl, diners hand-pinch the seasonings, since spoons for this are seldom provided. Pozole arrives in three colors:

- *Pozole Blanco* (poh SOH leh BLAN koh). White pozole. Nayarit features white pozole in a white brothy sauce.
- *Pozole Rojo* (poh SOH leh ROH hoh). Red pozole. Cooks in Jalisco state perfected this pozole simmering the ingredients in a red chile broth that's not picante.
- *Pozole Verde* (poh SOH leh BEHR deh). Green pozole. A specialty of Guerrero state, it's made with green chiles, Swiss chard, and ground pumpkin seeds. Chilapa, Guerrero, is famous for its pozole served on Thursdays, although there are better pozoles elsewhere. Acapulco, Guerrero, restaurants have made such a tradition of pozole Thursdays that many of them feature live entertainment with lots of singers, and often a flashy transvestite show. There, pozole diners choose among all three colors of pozole and the meal is accompanied with a large platter of botanas that's included in the price.

Quesadilla (keh sah DEE yah). Besides the uniform quesadilla made with a flour tortilla folded over cheese, in Chihuahua it's made with a corn tortilla and bathed in a green or red salsa. Colorful quesadillas in San Luis Potosí start with ground red ancho chiles mixed in the masa dough. Each quesadilla is formed and filled with white cheese and a slice of serrano chile. (See also *Molotes* above and Menu Primer A to Z: *Quesadilla*.)

Queso (KEH soh). Cheese. Though cheese making all over Mexico is a cottage and commercial industry, some regions, such as Oaxaca, Chiapas, Michoacán, Querétaro, and Chihuahua are especially well known for their varied production. As with Chihuahua cheese and that of Cotija, Michoacán, some of the cheeses from these regions make their way to stores throughout the country. However, an exploration of cheeses at the source reveals an even larger variety known and used only in that region.

A walk through the Mercado Abastos in Oaxaca City unveils a plethora of cheeses packed in wooden hoops, in round balls, and flat. The most famous of Oaxaca's cheese is probably white *quesillo* (keh SEE yoh), "rope" cheese. Etla, a town north of Oaxaca City, is devoted to making cheese and piles of it are available in the Wednesday market there.

Chiapas can be divided into four cheese regions: Rayon, Cintalapa/Tuxtla Gutiérrez, Ocosingo, and Pijijiapan. The excellent spongy Rayon cheese is sold by order only within the state.

Cattle production in Querétaro gives rise to a cheese-making industry and a wine and cheese fair near Tequisquiapan each May. Sleuthing cheese to its source is reason enough to travel in Mexico but most cheese is unpasteurized. (See also *Queso* entries in Menu Primer A to Z and Market Buying Tips.)

Relleno Negro (reh YEH noh NEH groh). A blackened chile sauce. (See also *Pavo* above, Menu Primer A to Z: *Chilmole,* and Market Buying Tips: *Chilmole.*)

Romeritos (roh meh REE tohs). Romeritos, a dish served at Easter and Christmas, is rather peculiar in taste. Its wizard's brew of ingredients include dried shrimp, mole, and potatoes flavored with romeritos, an herb that looks like rosemary but is blander in taste. Enjoying romeritos may require practice.

Sábana (SAH bah nah). A thin cut of beef. This northern Mexico specialty literally means "sheet," which is a clue to the thinness of the meat. Sábana is served with beans and perhaps rice and a salad.

Salpicón (sahl pee KOHN). Shredded marinated meat. A northern Mexico specialty, it's used in salads, stews, and tacos.

Salsa de Chicharrón (SAHL sah deh chee cha RROHN). Fried pork rind served in a thin, smooth tomato and dried chile sauce. A specialty of the state of Veracruz, it isn't a salsa in the traditional sense. Rather, large pieces of fried pork rind are cooked in the sauce and served together on a plate.

Sopa (SOH pah). Soup. Mexicans excel at making delicious fresh soups. Some are served more in one region than another and of course may cross regional lines. Such is the fate of the vegetable Sopa Tlalpeña that originated in Tlalpan, south of Mexico City. Soup or caldo by that name is served all over Mexico. (See also Menu Primer A to Z: *Sopa/ Sopa Tlalpeño.*)

Here are a few specialty soups from particular states or regions:

- *Caldo michi* (KAHL doh MEE chee). Catfish soup. A favorite around Lake Chapala, south of Guadalajara, it is made with catfish floating in vegetables and broth. Guanajuato cooks make a similar soup.

- *Moros con cristianos* (MOH rohs kohn krees tee YAH nohs). A Veracruz soup, meaning warring Moors and Christians, commingles black beans, rice, and epazote that float in a broth crowned with fried bananas.

- *Sopa de lima* (SOH pah deh LEE mah). Lime soup. A favorite soup in the Yucatán Peninsula isn't quite as tart as it may sound. It's a basic chicken broth seasoned with fresh lime juice and floating with bits of cilantro, tomato, finely shredded chicken, and strips of fried tortilla.

- *Sopa de pan* (SOH pah deh pahn). Bread soup from Chiapas. Though it's name indicates it's a soup, it isn't brothy or watery the way we think of soup. This filling festival food combines toasted French bread, onion, saffron, green beans, carrots, zucchini, banana, raisins, and hard-boiled eggs all together in chicken broth that's cooked until the broth isn't visible.

- *Sopa Poblana* (SOH pah poh BLAH nah). From the state of Puebla, this noble soup combines yellow/orange-colored, fragile blossoms of squash, chopped zucchini, and/or peas and chayote, with mushrooms, roasted chile poblano, garlic, onion, corn, and chicken broth. It's served garnished with cheese.

- *Sopa de sesos* (SOH pah deh SEH sohs). Brain soup. Though you may find brain soup elsewhere, restaurants in Mexico City seem to serve it more than most places.
- *Sopa Tarasca* (SOH pah tah RAHS kah). Tarascan, also called Purépecha, Indians make up the indigenous culture of the state of Michoacán and provide the same name for two popular soups—Sopa Tarasca. One is a tomato-based soup and the other is based on pureed pinto beans. However, both contain chicken broth, onions, garlic, and chiles and are garnished with cheese and slender fried tortilla strips. Neither is picante.
- *Sopa Tlaxcala* (SOH pah tlahks KAH lah). Served primarily in the state of Tlaxcala, this state's soup uses fried ground corn in a creamy soup to which squash blossoms, peas, and nopal cactus slices may be added.
- *Sopa tortilla* (SOH pah tohr TEE yah). The tomato-based sopa tarasca (see above) is sopa tortilla by another name.

(See also other soup-like dishes such as *Birria, Caldos, Clemole, Menudo,* and *Pozole* above and in the Menu Primer.)

Tacos (TAH kohs). Tacos. The darling of Mexican fast-food restaurants outside of Mexico has more variations in the country of its origin than any foreign taco king has yet to envision. Besides the special tacos mentioned below, *taquerías* (tah keh REE ahs), which are restaurants or pushcarts specializing in tacos, on Mexico's Baja Peninsula also produce delicious breaded fish tacos with an assortment of toppings including thick, rich cream, salsa, onions, cilantro, and fresh chopped tomatoes. From gleaming white carts, taco vendors in the Pátzcuaro market sell tacos made from all parts of the cow. (Besides the following, see also Menu Primer A to Z: *Tacos*.)

- *Tacos dorados* (TAH kohs doh RAH dohs). Aguascalientes cooks soar this otherwise mundane fried tube-shaped taco to the skies. First, rather than the common ground-chicken filling, these may come stuffed with pork or other meat mixture flavored with chiles, potatoes, raisins, olives, and capers. They are then covered with a tangy tomato sauce with side condiments to add such as cabbage, onions, chiles, oil, and vinegar.

- *Tacos de mantarraya* (TAH kohs deh mahn tah RRAH yah). On the Pacific Coast and Baja Peninsula restaurants may feature tacos made from the giant fluttering manta ray, one of the more curious inhabitants of Mexico's underwater world.

- *Tacos verbena* (TAH kohs behr BEH nah). A specialty of Puebla, these tacos take on the color of the Mexican flag with fillings of chicken and green chiles topped with a red sauce and white cream.

Tamales (tah MAH lehs). Masa (cornmeal dough), containing meat or a sweet flavoring, that's steamed in a corn husk, banana, or corn leaf. Tamal (tah MAHL) is the word for one. Two or more are called tamales. Before we begin this tour of Mexico's prodigious variety of tamales, I should mention that the wrapper isn't consumed. Corn husks and corn leaves are set aside. A tamal in a banana leaf can be sliced open in the middle, which is less messy than unwrapping.

Chiapas. The state of Chiapas has some of the best tamales. Travelers there will find at least twelve different kinds, many of which are as large or larger than a fifty-cent piece around—try them all.

Northern Mexico. The ubiquitous two-finger-wide and five-inch-long corn husk–wrapped tamal of northern Mexico, with a thin sliver of meat inside, is probably the best known outside the country. But they are by no means the best. (The canned version on U. S. grocery shelves should not be used for comparison.)

Oaxaca. Once in Mexico, the small hand-wide rather flatish tamal of Oaxaca is the one tourists speak about the most. Chicken and mole sauce flavor the center and it's steamed in a banana leaf wrapper. (See also Menu Primer A to Z: *Tamal* and Market Buying Tips: *Pepita Blanco* and *Achiote/ Achiote Preparado*.)

• *Brazo de Reina* (BRAH soh deh REH nah). Yucatán cooks present the brazo de reina, which means "arm of the queen." These large, long, filling tamales are made with chopped chaya leaf mixed in the dough, which is then filled with hard-boiled egg and roasted and ground melon seeds, and wrapped in a banana leaf to steam. The roasted melon seeds, called pepita blanco (peh PEE tah BLAHN koh), lend a peanut flavor to this tamal. The chaya is a spinach substitute, but the cooked flavor is mild compared to cooked spinach. The tamal is served sliced, showing off its interior swirly design of molded ingredients. A special mild red sauce adds a twist of flavor. Other Yucatecan tamales resemble the brazo de reina in ingredients but have different names.

- *Colado* (koh LAH doh). This large, delicious, Campeche tamal, steamed in a banana leaf, contains chicken, chopped onion and tomato, and a hint of epazote.

- *Corunda* (koh ROON dah). A triangular-shaped tamal from the state of Michoacán is steamed in a wrapping of fresh green corn leaves and may have a hunk of pork inside. *Corundas de ceniza* (koh ROON dahs deh seh NEE sah) are made from corn boiled in wood ashes, which impart a special delicious flavor. A drizzle of sour cream or a red chile sauce completes the corunda. The freshest, most delicious, and least expensive corundas are sold mornings by women around the plazas in Pátzcuaro. Tall aluminum-lidded pots keep these delicate tamales piping hot until they sell out about mid-morning. Women such as these supply corundas to area restaurants where they are sold for much more.

- *Muk bil pollo* (mook beel POH yoh). A huge, achiote-seasoned tamal that's a specialty of Quintana Roo during the Days of the Dead, November 1–2. Achiote-flavored masa dough is filled with cooked chicken, pork, or turkey and covered in a exotic sauce created from garlic, oregano, onion, chiles, epazote, tomato, and vinegar. It's cooked in an earthen pit.

- *Tamales de frijol* (tah MAH lehs deh FREE hohl). Bean tamales. Temoac, a village in eastern Morelos state, makes bean-filled tamales only for the Days of the Dead.

- *Uchepo* (ooh CHEH poh). The five-inch-long uchepo, a specialty of Michoacán, can be either sweet with the flavor of strawberries or another fruit, or hold a tender piece of pork inside, and be spiced with poblano pepper.

- *Zacahuil* (sah kah WEEL). Veracruz is famous for its huge and extremely delicious zacahuil. Meat of a whole cooked pork leg, doused with a special chile and tomato sauce, is covered in masa, wrapped in a banana leaf, and baked in an earthen pit. Another Veracruz version of the zacahuil is the tamal de olla (tah MAHL deh OH yah), or pot tamal, because it's cooked in a large deep pot. It's just as tasty as the pit-baked version. If you're in Mexico City and not Veracruz, a few vendors at the outdoor part of the Sunday Lagunilla Market sell zacahuil.

Tasajo (tah SAH hoh). A large, thin piece of salted meat. It's a specialty in both Oaxaca and Chiapas and similar to cecina, which is a Morelos state specialty. A meal of tasajo may be accompanied by beans, tortillas, and rice and perhaps a small salad.

Tik-n-xic (teek en CHEEK). A specialty of the Yucatán Peninsula, red snapper is butterflied, rubbed with achiote preparada, dotted with sliced tomatoes, onions, and garlic, and grilled on an open wood fire. The subtle flavors blend harmoniously, creating a delicious meal that's not picante. (See also *Achiote Preparada* entries in Menu Primer A to Z and Market Buying Tips.)

Tinga (TEEN gah). A special Puebla beef stew. The basic recipe calls for shredded beef, invigorated with onions, garlic, tomatoes, chiles, and potatoes. The deluxe version includes fried longaniza (sausage) and at serving the whole mixture is topped with slices of avocado and rings of white onion.

Tinquinipaal (teen keen EE pahl). Shark pâté. Ground shark meat is mixed with spices and chiles and served as a botana. (See also *Cazón* above.)

Torta (TOHR tah). Sandwich or fried patty. In most places a torta is a sandwich. But in some places a torta has nothing to do with being a sandwich. In Acapulco a torta de papa (TOHR tah deh PAH pa) is a fried cheese and potato patty. (For regional variations on the torta as a sandwich see also *Chanclas, Lonche, Pambazo,* and *Cemita* above.)

Tortilla (tohr TEE yah). A round corn or wheat flour flat bread. But this ancient Mexican staple goes well beyond simple yellow or white corn and wheat flour and extends the boundaries of the common five-inch tortillas. Blue corn, once the domain of peasant food, has found its way to gourmet tables as has red corn in the making of tortillas. The pleasing color coordination of a blue corn tortilla holding red salsa or pink shrimp, avocados, and salsa is an artist's delight.

- *Blandita* (blahn DEE tah). A thin corn tortilla sold fresh in Oaxaca City food markets.
- *Pellizcada* (peh yeez KAH dah). In Veracruz the pellizcada is a thickish corn tortilla, made of masa and lard. The crimped top of the tortilla vaguely resembles a gathered skirt that's been dropped. This heavy regional tortilla can be very salty and thick, but also filling and delicious. It's served with black beans and fried bananas, or with a green or red sauce, or plain as an accompaniment to any meal. A *pellizcada compuesta* (peh yeez KAH dah kohm PWEHS tah) is a pellizcada served with smoked pork and black beans.
- *Tlayuda* (tlah YOOH dah). In Oaxaca, market vendors cry "tlayuda, tlayuda" to hawk these platter-size tortillas. Leathery in consistency, and delicious to the taste, they are used by the peas-

ant populace as an edible plate capable of holding a meal. Occasionally restaurants serve it as an example of regional food. It's also spelled *clayuda* (clah YOOH dah).

- *Totopo* (toh TOH poh). In Oaxaca a totopo is a thick, hard, puffy tortilla punched with holes. Elsewhere a totopo is a wedge of corn tortilla that's been baked or deep-fried and is used as a scooper for refried beans or guacamole.

Zacahuil (sah kah WEEL). See also *Tamales* above.

MARKET BUYING TIPS
· ◨ ·

Mexican food stores come in three basic types:
The most plentiful is the neighborhood grocery
called *aborrote* (ah boh ROH teh) or simply *tienda*
(tee YEHN dah), which means store. It may be a
closet-sized room selling a small assortment of
snacks and soft drinks and essentials such as bread,
milk, and cheese. Or a larger aborrote will offer a
wide assortment of basic necessities such as canned
pickled chiles, condiments, cereal, baby food, peanut butter, packaged table and sweet bread, rice,
bottled water and diapers, etc. Many aborrotes
shelve their merchandise behind a counter; clients
request food items from what they see or what may
be in a back room. Larger aborrotes have shelves
and aisles, like a mini supermarket.

More elaborate is the supermarket or *super mercado* (SOO pehr mehr KAH doh), which is very similar to supermarkets in the United States. There, a
full complement of packaged and prepared foods is
available, with one exception—frozen food. Frozen

food in Mexico isn't as well accepted as it is else-where, so there's not much of it.

Finally, there's the ancient and very typical open-air market where everything from garbanzos to goats is available—fresh. Generally unavailable at open markets are all the packaged and canned goods sold in super mercados and abarrotes. Open markets are the most fascinating of all, both for the elaborate array of food, and for the social customs that take place there. What follows are items you may find useful as you travel, as gifts, or as a pleasurable memento of your journey.

Achiote/Achiote Preparado (ah CHEE oh teh/ah CHEE oh teh preh pah RAH doh). Once you've discovered achiote (the seed of the annatto tree) and the beguiling flavor of *achiote preparado* (the fabulously aromatic prepared paste made from the ground seed), a quest for take-home may ensue. Open markets in the Yucatán Peninsula will uniformly carry both the packaged and freshly made paste, seeds, and ground seed. Small packages of achiote can also be found in markets outside that area, but the quest may take patience. All forms can be found in the Mercado Merced in Mexico City. If your itinerary permits finding it late in your travels, wait to buy it then, since it can be a weighty purchase.

The seeds, or *semillas* (seh MEE yahs) in Spanish, are not as easily found as the paste. The dry, ground form (before other seasonings are added) has a rich, slightly nutty flavor and is used to flavor soups and to give them a deep red color, to mix with masa for tamales, or to make achiote preparado. The prepared seasoning (a meritorious mixture of ground achiote seeds mixed with wheat and corn flour, garlic, salt, cumin, cinnamon, and oregano—ah the aroma) is used by cooks throughout the Yucatán as a marinade on baked or grilled chicken, fish, and pork. Achiote preparado is also the central flavoring in *tik-n-xic* (teek ehn CHEEK), and both pollo (chicken) and cochinita (pork) pibil.

Cooks in the Yucatán make a thick/soupy consistency of the paste by adding sour orange juice. This large orange, called *naranjo agrio* (nah RAHN hoh AH gree yoh), is lemony but has the faint smell of an orange. Since sour oranges aren't available north of the border, the combination of fresh grapefruit or lemon juice and fresh orange juice also works. Vinegar is an accepted and delicious substitute. Experiment with different white vinegars. Keep the powdered version tightly sealed in a dry place. The paste will keep frozen for years.

Adobo (ah DOH boh). A meat seasoning. The dry ingredients of adobo are often found bottled and labled "adobo" in the grocery store spice section. Ingredients include ground ancho chile, onion, garlic, cloves, cinnamon, coriander, salt, and pepper. At cooking time, tomatoes, oil, and chicken broth are added to the dry ingredients. For a more authentic purchase, venture into a Mexican fresh food market (not a supermarket) and head for the section selling moles and other prepared pastes. In that section the local adobo paste will be mounded along with all other pastes and sold by every imaginable fraction of a kilo. Double wrap it in plastic and it'll travel well. It keeps indefinitely in the refrigerator or freezer.

Aguas Frescas (AHG wahs FREHS kahs). Fruit waters. Most are easily made with oranges, limes, and watermelon mixed with sugar and water. More difficult are horchata, made with ground rice or melon seeds, and jamaica, made with a dried part of a particular flower. Jamaica isn't made with dried hibiscus flowers as is commonly thought. These last two are sold bottled in concentrated form. Don Manuel is one of several brands.

Alegría (ah leh GREE ah). A sweet hard bar or round cake snack that looks like molded birdseed. It's made of nutritious amaranth seeds held together with honey or brown sugar and water. It's sold packaged at newsstands, markets, and grocery stores. (See also *Amaranto* below.)

Amaranto (ah mah RAHN toh). Amaranth. A lysine-rich pre-Conquest grain, its cultivation was forbidden by Spain because of its use in Aztec rituals. Lysine is an essential amino acid not ordinarily found in plant food. Cultivated in Mexico today, amaranth is made into snack cakes, cereal, noodles, sweet alegría cakes, a hot drink mixed with milk and chocolate, and pinole (a finely ground mixture of toasted corn and brown sugar), to name a few items. You may find the snack cakes, noodles, and cereals on grocery shelves, but the fine powder is almost always an open-air market purchase. A February festival honors the grain in Xochimilco near Mexico City. (See also *Alegría* above and Menu Primer A to Z: *Pinole*.)

Atole (ah TOH leh). The traditional morning and evening drink made from ground melon or rice is packaged and sold under the Maizena brand in all grocery stores.

Barro (BAHR roh). Clay. (See also *Ollas de Barro* below.)

Café (kah FEH). Coffee. Grown in six Mexican states, fresh roasted beans are available for purchase in most towns. Sold by the kilo or half kilo, you'll find especially rich-tasting coffee in the states of Chiapas and Veracruz.

Cajeta (kah heh tah). Carmelized cow's or goat's milk. You've oohed over it in crepes and churros, and reveled in its rich flavor in ice cream. Now you want to tote some home. Large jars of it are sold in grocery stores. It's another of those weighty indulgences.

Cal (kahl). Lime slake. Sold in white rocky chunks all over Mexico, it's used to condition a clay comal. The clay comal, used for frying tortillas and browning peppers, must be conditioned with cal before each use.

Caldo de pollo (KAHL doy deh POH yoh). Chicken bouillon. Look for the tasty Knoor brand of granular chicken bouillon that even the purest of Mexican cooks use as a substitute for homemade chicken broth.

Canasta (kah NAHS tah). Basket. Basket weaving is a cottage industry in Mexico and handsome baskets are sold everywhere. They come plain without adornment, woven of colored reeds, or with yarn designs on top. They grow on you. But ah, the variety. Shops selling baskets are called *cesterías* (sehs teh REE ahs) in some places; however, baskets of all kinds are most easily found in open-air markets. *Cesto* (SEHS toh) is another word for basket.

The *chiquihuite* (chee kee WEE teh), the classically beautiful basket of pre-Hispanic design, is sold most widely in markets in central Mexico. It's favored by fresh tortilla and tamale vendors everywhere. Woven from a stiff, wide reed, it's sold in its natural color of pale blond. Its double thickness keeps food warm and it comes in many sizes. Besides being great tortilla or roll servers, they make beautiful plant holders.

Basket-making also flourishes in the Yucatán Peninsula where weavers create palm leaf baskets woven in damp caves.

Basket weavers from a village near Taxco take thousands of their large and small colorful baskets all over the country.

In the chocolate-growing region near Villahermosa, small willow baskets are the same shape of larger ones used in the field for dumping chocolate seeds directly from their hard outer shell. In the Copper Canyon, Tarahumara Indian women sell a variety of baskets made from sotol leaves.

Cesto (SEHS toh). Basket. See also *Canasta* above.

Cheez Whiz (cheez wheez). Cheez Whiz. The same brand and small size of spreadable processed cheese that's sold in the United States is found in grocery stores in Mexico. It's useful when you want to pack a picnic lunch that won't spoil before you eat it, or to prepare a quick in-room snack. Local bread, mayonnaise, and fresh sliced avocado dress it admirably.

Chiles (CHEE lehs). Chiles. Ah, the smoky fragrance of dried chiles mounded in market stalls. It's enough to make you want to go wild creating Mexican sauces. Those who really get into peppers may feel compelled to stash some in their luggage. U.S. Customs allows you to bring in enough of the dried variety in sufficient quantity for thirty days personal use. Obviously that's open to interpretation, so use your judgment and be sure to declare it upon arrival in the United States.

Buying chiles is a learning process that every diehard chile aficionado faces. Though the chiles described in the Menu Primer A to Z are the names commonly used for the chiles, there are sometimes local names for the same chiles, or an area may dub a chile by a name already used for another chile elsewhere, all of which can be very confusing for the shopper. If you dead-end into that problem and you think there's a chile you might want but can't identify, buy it, label the chile with the local name, and try to solve the confusion later. To avoid chile confusion at home, bring along sealable quart-size plastic bags and label them as you buy.

Some recipes call for a dozen of one kind of fresh or dried chile, but many recipes call for only two or three fresh or dried chiles (though the recipe may use two or three *each* of two or three different kinds), so plan your stash accordingly.

Dried chiles aren't as fragile as they look. In fact they should be as pliable as well-tanned leather. Pliability is a sign of being freshly dried; if a pepper crumbles in your hand, it's too old.

Since chiles can burn hands and eyes, handle them carefully, and in the kitchen use plastic gloves. The heat of chiles comes from the veins inside as well as the seeds. Deflame them by removing the veins and seeds. The intensity of chile pepper heat is also determined by the soil in which the chiles are grown. Thus, the same chile bought in one area of Mexico may be more, or less, hot than one purchased in another region.

A plastic bag is all right for transport of dried chiles but never for long storage. Store dried varieties in a dry place in tightly lidded glass jars. Fresh peppers should be stored in the refrigerator in a paper rather than a plastic bag. Washing won't harm dried peppers (in fact it's recommended since they've been through many hands), but wait to do it just before using them.

Of the dried chiles mentioned in the Menu Primer A to Z, the most often called for are the ancho, arbol, chipotle, guajillo, mulatto, and pasilla.

Many chiles are also bottled as hot sauce under a variety of names and are readily available on grocery shelves. Salsa Búfalo and Valentia are two good all-purpose salsas that are not too picante. The canned version of the sliced marinated chiles and vegetables is also sold in every grocery store in Mexico and may have escabeche (pickled) on the label. Costeña is one brand with a combination of pickled vegetables and chiles. The profound abundance and variety of peppers are particularly pronounced in the Mercado Abastos in Oaxaca City and the Mercado Merced in Mexico City. (For a description of dried chiles, see Menu Primer A to Z.)

Chilmole (cheel MOH leh). A savory paste made from blackened chiles, onions, garlic, and achiote. It's also called *relleno negro* (reh YEH noh NEH groh), *recado negro* (reh KAH doh NEH groh), and *chirmole* (cheer MOH leh). The paste is sold fresh in markets and packaged in boxes. It keeps for a year or more in the refrigerator. Mix it with water or chicken broth for cooking turkey, rabbit, pork, beef, and chicken.

Chocolate (cho koh LAH teh). Chocolate. It's spelled the same as in English, but it's pronounced differently in Mexico. Vendors sell it freshly ground and mixed with almonds, sugar, and cinnamon in Oaxaca, and in presweetened cakes. Near Villahermosa, visitors can follow a chocolate route visiting cacao (chocolate) plantations and shops selling homemade chocolate. All grocery stores in Mexico sell commercially prepared packages of it too, and there's nothing better to bring back the memories of Mexico than Mexican hot chocolate brewed on your own home turf. (See also *Chocolate* entries in Menu Primer A to Z and Regional/Seasonal Specialties.)

Comal (koh MAHL). Clay or tin frying platter. The big round clay disks have been used since pre-Hispanic days for preparing tortillas and browning peppers. Before using each time, however, the clay comal must be conditioned with cal, which can also be bought in the market. (See also *Cal* above.) Tin comals are also widely sold and used. Though they rust and warp, they still have life long after they look ugly. A tin comal with a flat rim and well or indented middle is called a *comal de pozo* (koh MAHL deh POH soh), or "well" comal. It's used much like a wok, frying in the bowl-like well, and resting finished pieces on the rim. These are sold in huge street vendor sizes and in sizes small enough for a stove top.

Crema de Cacahuate (KREH mah deh kah kah WAH teh). Peanut butter. Familiar U.S. brands and Mexican brands are found in supermarkets and abarrotes. (Peanut butter is also called *Mantequilla de Cacahuate*.)

Cucharero (koo cha REH roh). A small wall shelf with drilled holes for hanging wooden spoons. These decorative staples of the Mexican kitchen may be more easily found in a shop featuring artesanias or crafts. However, unfinished ones may be found in open-air markets. (See also *Repisa* below.)

Dulce/Dulces (DOOL seh/DOOL sehs). Sweets. The staggering variety of packaged and prepared sweets in Mexico is amazing. So venture forth among the wildly mysterious kinds of sweets armed with the names of a few. Below is a starter list many of which make great gifts and are packaged for gift giving. (Besides these see also Regional/Seasonal Specialties: *Dulces* and Menu Primer A to Z: *Dulce*.)

- *Alegría* (ah leh GREE ah). An amaranth cake snack. The ancient Mexican grain amaranth is formed into round disks and squares and held together with honey or boiled sugar water. Sometimes nuts are added or decorate the top. Around the Days of the Dead (November 1–2), it's formed into skulls and peanuts and raisins make the eyes, nose, and mouth.
- *Ate* (AH teh). An outrageously sweet fruit paste that's sturdy enough to cut. It's served with a mild, sliced white cheese as a dessert.

- *Borrachos* (boh RRAH chohs). Wine candy rolled in sugar. It comes in many colors that all taste the same.
- *Camote* (kah MOH teh). Sugar crystallized pumpkin.
- *Camotes de puebla* (kah MOH tehs deh Pweh blah). Sugarized squash and fruits, rolled into tubes and packaged a dozen to the box.
- *Chilacayote* (CHEEL ah kah YOH teh). A bright green crystallized squash.
- *Cocadas* (koh KAH dahs). Coconut bars or squares which, during festivals, may be colored red, white, and green—Mexico's national colors.
- *Domingueras* (doh min GWEH rahs). A bright yellow disk, made of pineapple and adorned with roasted coconut.
- *Dulce de alfajor* (DOOL seh deh al fah HOHR). Layers of bright pink and white pudding-like coconut-flavored cake make this an especially festive-looking selection.
- *Dulce de leche* (DOOL seh deh LEH cheh). Milk candy. Milk candy is also divided by names for particular candies. It comes in ridged tube shapes, round with a nut on top, and somewhat star-shaped. Of the milk candies, *Jamoncillos* (hah mohn SEE yohs) are milk candy sweets with nuts while rose-colored milk candy is called *piñón* (peen YOHN); *pepita* (peh PEE tah) is red on the top and milky brown on the bottom.
- *Higos* (HEE gohs). Figs crystallized in sugar.
- *Limon* (lee MOHN). It looks like a lime that has

been stuffed with shredded coconut—and it is. The shell of the bright green lime is cut in half, crystallized with the center removed, and then filled with shredded coconut.

- *Manzanas* (mahn SAH nahs). Crystallized apples.
- *Morillanas* (moh ree YAH nahs). A combination of peanuts, milk, and sugar that creates a thin fritter, or a cookie-like disk.
- *Mueganos* (MWEH gah nohs). Wheat flour and sugar formed into small balls. The balls are slightly mashed together to create a baseball-sized lumpy-looking ball that's rolled in cinnamon and sugar. The finished product resembles a popcorn ball.
- *Palonqueta* (pah lohn KEH tah). Made from either pumpkin seeds or peanuts held together with boiled sugar water or honey.
- *Peras* (PEH rahs). Crystallized pears.
- *Tamarindo con chile* (tah mah REEN doh kohn CHEE leh). This combination marries sweetened tamarand seeds with chile for a snack that's not *picante* (spicy hot). It may also be made without chile. Tamarand sweets appear shaped into tubes, as flat and round, and in balls rolled in sugar.
- *Tortita de Santa Clara* (tohr TEE tah deh SAHN tah KLAH rah). A delightful cookie made of flour, champurrado (chocolate atole), pepitas, and sugar.

Epazote (eh pah SOH teh). Wormseed. This pungent herb is finding its way into requesón for a quesadilla filling and alta cocina cooks have tamed its strong flavor for use in sauces for fish. But traditionally, Mexican cooks believe that a pot of black beans isn't complete without at least 1/4 cup fresh epazote, and that a quesadilla isn't really flavored properly without a sprig of epazote. If you're a believer then you'll want to hunt up some seeds, which in Spanish is semillas (seh MEE yahs). Your local herb market at home may have the plant or seed. But one warning: it's a weed and grows like one. However, it's very easy to pull up if it threatens to take over your garden. One plant will be enough for a lifetime. The flavor changes when it's dried, but it's still good for use in beans. It's often suggested as a substitute for yerba santa, an oft-used herb in Mexican cooking, but difficult to find outside of Mexico. However, its taste really cannot be duplicated by any other herb. (See also Menu Primer A to Z: *Epazote*.)

Especias (ehs PEH see yahs). Spices. Browse through the spice section of any grocery store for bottled spices you may not find at home. Open-air markets also present them in their unpackaged dry form.

Flan (flahn). Egg custard. This stalwart of the Mexican dessert menu comes boxed and sold in Mexican supermarkets.

Fruta (FROOH tah). Fruit. Fresh peelable fruit such as mandarin oranges, bananas, and other fruit are abundant in open markets and very inexpensive. For health reasons eat only peeled fruit.

Galleta (gah YEH tah). Cookie or cracker. Mexico has a good, though not large, assortment of crackers that go well with cheese, peanut butter, and soup.

Hoja de Maguey (OH hah deh MAH geh). Maguey paper. Thin parchment paper is made from the leaf of the maguey plant and used for wrapping mixiotes. It's sold primarily in markets in Tlaxcala, Puebla, near Teotihacán, and in Mexico City's *Mercado* (mehr KAH doh) Merced (Merced Market). It's heavy and bulky though, so save its purchase until just before heading home. Plastic bags called *bolsas plasticas para mixiotes* (BOHL sahs PLAHS tee kahs PAH rah mee SHOH tehs) especially for steaming mixiotes are also sold in these regions. While not the real thing, the plastic bags may be more efficient to tote.

Hoja de Maíz (OH hahs deh mah EEZ). Dried corn husk. Used to wrap steamed tamales. These are readily available in packages in open markets or grocery stores.

Hoja de Platano (OH hah deh PLAH tah noh). Banana leaf. Used as a wrapper for tamales and pit- or oven-baked meat, it's sold fresh and folded in squares in open markets.

Hojas de Aguacate (OH hahs deh ah wah KAH teh). Avocado leaves. The lightly fragrant leaf of the Mexican avocado tree is used in many sauces and pit-baked meat. It's found both dried and fresh in markets. Avocado trees grown elsewhere don't produce the same flavor in the leaf and aren't recommended for cooking.

Huevos (WEH bohs). Eggs. A little throat clearing is in order. To avoid an embarrassing moment, there's a little matter of how to ask for eggs. *"¿Tiene huevos?"* (tee YEHN eh WEH bohs) is asking if the person has human testicles. Huevos is the slang for this term. Fewer stifled laughs, grins, and downright snickers will occur if you use the phrase *"¿Hay huevos?"* (I WEH bohs), meaning "Are there eggs?" Eggs are purchased individually and piled loose into a plastic bag, which the purchaser must then manage to carry home carefully. (See also Comfort Foods: *Eggs* and Menu Primer A to Z: *Huevos.*)

Jícama (HEE kah mah). Jicama. This crunchy turnip/potato–looking tuber that tastes vaguely like a cross between a potato and coconut makes a peelable vegetable for a picnic or snack. Peeled and sliced in long strips, it's served the way you would sliced celery on a fresh vegetable plate.

Jícara (HEE kah rah). A gourd used as a serving utensil. Throughout Mexico natural gourds are used as soup bowls (in a country market perhaps), scoops, tortilla servers, storage containers, measuring bowls, and water canteens. Ambulatory vendors laden with gourds to sell sometimes appear at festivals, but gourds may also be found in markets.

Jugo (HOOH goh). Juice. Though excellent fresh juices are easily found in Mexico, fine canned ones are available in super mercados, especially the Jumex brand. As for a utensil to squeeze your own, handheld metal juice squeezers are found in open markets. Sizes are small enough to accommodate limes, mid-sized for oranges, and huge to handle a large sour orange or a grapefruit.

Kahlúa (kah LOO ah). Coffee liqueur. This is one of the most popular take-home gifts. It's mixed with coffee or with milk and served over ice with vodka and rum. Dribble it over ice cream or blend it with ice cream for a thick drink. Recipes are on the bottle. (See also Beverages A to Z: *Liqueurs/Kahlúa.*)

Laurel (lah ooh REHL). Bay leaves. Mexican bay leaves are small, thin, roundish and a bit milder in taste than the long Mediterranean bay leaves sold in the United States.

Leche Seco (LEH cheh SEH koh). Powdered milk. Mexico's dry milk is much better flavored than any in the United States. Nido brand is sweet and excellent.

Mandarina (mahn dah REE nah). Tangerine. Like oranges, tangerines are sold in great piles in most Mexican markets—you buy by the *montón* (mohn TOHN) or mountain, usually six to eight tangerines for the quoted price.

Mantequilla de Cacahuate (mahn teh KEE yah deh kah kah WAH teh). Peanut butter. (See also *Crema de Cacahuate* above.)

Masa de Maíz/Masa de Harina (MAH sah deh mah EEZ/MAH sah deh ah REE nah). Corn flour/wheat flour. Used for making corn and flour tortillas, both are sold packaged in Mexican supermarkets.

Mayonesa (mah oh NEH sah). Mayonnaise. Since Mexican mayonnaise has a slight hint of fresh lime, it makes a great addition to sandwiches or salads and is a good gift to take home. It's sold under the McCormick and Hellman labels and comes in an easily packable small size as well as one intended to serve a crowd.

Molcajete (mohl kah HEH teh). A three-legged grinding bowl with pestle. Once made of volcanic stone, today those formed of rough concrete are the most often sold. It's excellent for grinding spices, and for some spices the molcajete works better than an electric grinder. Also sold for the same purpose, but not useful, are clay bowls with a scored bottom on the inside of the bowl. The clay chips off and gets into the food.

Mole (MOH leh). If you become smitten with this pungent sauce, it's easy to find freshly made in local open markets or in jars on supermarket shelves. In local markets, huge mounds of fresh mole paste, in all its glorious colors and fabulous aromas, are sold by the kilo (or increments thereof). To select the best one for you, do a discreet sniff test, or ask a local which mole is a favorite. It's usually scooped into a fresh plastic bag, but ask for two bags for a double wrap, to keep it fresh and contained until you arrive home. It freezes well for up to a year—maybe longer. Mole in jars should be kept in a refrigerator after opening. Add chicken broth to the purchased paste for a thickish soup consistency. (See also *mole* entries in Menu Primer A to Z and Regional/Seasonal Specialties.)

Molinillo (moh lee NEE yoh). A carved wooden chocolate beater. Most tourists won't use this hand-carved beater for chocolate. Instead these beaters wind up as decorative wall ornaments, especially in a collection showing all the different carvings. Some are simple and others have special designs and wooden rings, all of which are puzzling to contemplate since they are carved out of a single piece of wood. These are found in open-air markets with the wooden spoons and plastic bowls and pots.

Montón (mohn TOHN). A heap, a pile, or, literally, mountain-shaped. In markets fruits are often sold by the montón, say six or eight mandarin oranges or potatoes piled neatly in a mountain or pyramid shape for a certain price.

Ollas de Barro (OH yahs deh BAH rroh). Clay pots. Mexico's captivating array of clay cooking pots can bring on a desire to carry them home. Some are glazed with lead glazes and others are plain. Mexican cooks cure the pots by boiling them in water laced with plenty of garlic. Whether or not that gets rid of the lead in the glaze, I don't know. But the pots make great serving dishes for dry or nonacidic food even if you don't use them for frying or baking. To protect against the potentially harmful lead glaze (if you want to use them for serving), line the bowl with tortillas or lettuce, depending on what you're serving. Clay pots look great hanging on a wall, and alternately they're useful as a repository for mail or magazines, again depending on the size, and as pencil and plant holders. One particularly useful pot is the *olla nixtamal* (OH yah neex tah MAHL). It's a clay pot punched with multiple holes all over the base. It's used for making tortilla masa. Cooks soften corn kernels with lime and let the runoff drip through the holes of a nixtamal pot in preparation for making tortilla dough. These three-legged pots make great, atmospheric candle holders with the light flickering through the holes. Once the desire for clay pots sets in, thinking up what to do with them seems to be no problem.

Pan (pahn). Bread. It's sold in aborrotes, super mercados, and bakeries called *pastelerías/panaderías* (pahs teh leh REE ahs/pahn ah deh REE ahs). Like Mexico's cheese and chiles, hundreds of varieties of bread are produced in Mexico. Before settling for the common bolillo roll (which is very good) or sliced white Bimbo bread, check out local bakeries and the market for regional variations.

Mexican bakeries are arranged with multi-tiers of metal shelves lined up around the room and loaded, sometimes almost to the ceiling, with uncovered and unpackaged freshly baked goods. Some of these panaderías occupy enormous spaces with a staggering variety of offerings, others are small one-room affairs with an assortment of basic rolls, muffins, and bread. To get the hang of shopping in a Mexican bakery, do as the Mexicans do.

How to shop in a pastry shop/bakery: From open shelves the shopper, armed with a metal tray and tongs found upon entering, wanders about selecting from the dizzying assortment of rolls, muffins, Mexican-style cupcakes, savory and sweet breads, and cookies. When the shopper is either finished or exhausted from all the decisions, the tray of baked goodies is presented at the checkout counter. There, a clerk usually adds the total in his or her head and presents the amount to the cashier.

Baked goods are usually very inexpensive. But they

are seldom priced on the racks, so you usually have no way of knowing the cost of the delicacies you're choosing until the total is produced at the checkout.

One caveat: Mexican bakery products should be eaten the day they are purchased, since most will dry out and crumble quickly. Most bakeries bag goods in paper sacks, which don't keep these fragile baked goods fresh for long. Stash a good-sized plastic bag in your day pack for those sudden urges to purchase when passing a bakery displaying an irresistible assortment of baked goodies. (See also Menu Primer A to Z: *Pan* and *Boli-llio* and Regional/Seasonal Specialties: *Pan*.)

Pepita Blanco (peh PEE tah BLAHN koh). Ground roasted melon seeds. The aroma and taste is that of mild peanut butter. The seeds are sold freshly ground in markets primarily in the Yucatán Peninsula. It's used in making tamales and mole.

Piloncillo (pee lohn SEE yoh). Unrefined hard brown sugar. Sold in cone shapes in Mexican markets and required in many Mexican recipes. It's also a great gift for the died-in-the-wool Mexico connoisseur back home.

Pipián (pee pee YAHN). A green, *pipián verde* (BEHR deh), or red, *pipián rojo* (pee pee YAHN ROH hoh), sauce using roasted and ground melon, squash, and sesame seeds for taste and as a thickener. Pipiáns are considered moles.

The red version features ground seeds of achiote and roasted melon seeds. Red pipián paste is found frequently in Yucatecan markets. Green pipián is eaten frequently in Puebla and can be found in markets there. Look for the fresh pipián paste in the large open food markets in the section with moles and adobo. Pipián travels well, but be sure to double or triple bag it to prevent seepage. At home, cook it diluted with chicken broth. (See also Menu Primer A to Z: *Mole* and Regional/Seasonal Specialties: *Pipián*.)

Pollo en Polvo (POH yoh ehn POHL voh). Chicken bouillon. Store-bought Mexican bouillon is much tastier than its U.S. counterpart. It's used widely by Mexican cooks and is sold in every supermarket.

Queso (KEH soh). Cheese. Testing Mexico's cheese production is one of the delights of exploring the country. There are hundreds of varieties and many are made only for regional use. Every local open-air market features them. But do your marketing early in the day when the cheese is fresh—it won't be refrigerated in an open-air market. And sample gingerly, since tainted unpasteurized cheese can be the source of Montezuma's revenge or worse. Or shop at a grocery store where local cheese may be sold in refrigerated cases. An inexpensive and delicious meal can be concocted with fresh market cheese, a local bread, and sliced avocados and tomatoes. (For tips on varieties, regions, textures, uses, and flavors see also

Queso entries in the Menu Primer A to Z and Regional/Seasonal Specialties. And—even after all that's written here about wonderful Mexican cheese—see also *Cheez Whiz* above.)

Recado (reh KAH doh). A prepared mixture of spice ingredients ready to take home and cook. In markets, recados are the ready-made pastes of adobo, achiote preparado, mole, etc.

Repisa (reh PEE sah). A wall shelf. Mexican kitchens and other parts of the home often feature this single or multi-shelf unit. Usually a foot or a foot and a half wide, they may have intricate carvings on the back portion showing against the wall or be painted or lacquered colorfully. They make a nice showcase for a collection of salt shakers or a repository for kitchen spices. (See also *Cucharero* above.)

Rompope (rohm POH peh). An eggnog-like drink. The celebratory richness of Mexico's rum-laced rompope is bottled under several brands—all acceptable. It makes a handsome gift and is sold in both grocery and liquor stores.

Salsa Búfalo (SAHL sah BOOH fah loh). A mild bottled sauce that's set on tables as an added condiment for spicing a meal. Supermarkets sell it.

Sausa Maggi (sah OOH sah MAH gee). Maggi sauce. Mexico's answer to Worcestershire sauce is slightly different in taste. It's used in mixed drinks, in sauces, and as a marinade for grilled vegetables and fish.

Tejocote (teh hoh KOH teh). A fruit similar to a yellow apple.

Tequila (teh KEE lah). The distilled liquor made from the blue agave and featured in margaritas and other drinks. The best tequila is labeled 100 percent pure, without additives such as sugar. Excellent brands are Herradura, Patrón, El Tesoro de Don Felipe, and Chinaco. (See also Beverages A to Z: *Alcoholic Drinks / Tequila.*)

Tortilla Press. Heavy cast-iron tortilla presses, used for making corn tortillas, are sold in grocery stores and open-air markets. Blocky wooden ones are also sold and seem to have more character. If you buy the latter, inspect it to make sure the wood will press flat and that its hinges are sturdy.

Vino (BEEH noh). Wine. (See Beverages A to Z: *Alcoholic Drinks / Vino.*)

USEFUL WORDS
QUICK REFERENCE GUIDE
· ▦ ·

THIS SECTION is intended to provide some of the most useful words a diner may need to order a meal, a drink, explain a food request, find a particular food, ask for the check, or obtain the correct dining utensils.

Bakery. *Pastelería* (pahs teh leh ree ah)/*Panadería* (pahn ah deh REE yah). A pastelería will have a large assortment of elaborate cakes, and perhaps a selection of muffins, rolls, sweet breads, and cookies. A panadería offers everything except cakes and pies. (See also Market Buying Tips: *Pan.*)

Big. *Grande* (GRAHN deh). An important word to know for asking the size of a meal, a portion, or a margarita. The opposite is chico (CHEE koh), which means small. In between is *mediano* (meh dee YAH noh), meaning medium. Where language fails, waiters will usually gesture the size.

Bitter. *Amargo* (ah MAHR goh).

Bottle. *Botella* (boh TEH yah). If you want water in

a bottle, a soft drink in a bottle rather than a can, etc., then use this word.

Bunch. *Manojo* (mah NOH hoh). This handy word is useful to use with a handful or a bunch of cilantro, parsley, or napkins, etc.

Burn/Burned. *Quemar/Quemado* (keh MAHR/keh MAH doh). It rarely happens, but if something arrives burned, you'll want to communicate about it.

Carry Out/To Go. *Llevar* (yeh BAHR). Say *"para llevar"* (PAH rah yeh BAHR) if you want something to go, such as a sandwich, soft drink, pizza, or meal.

Check. *La Cuenta* (lah KWEN tah). This word is used to ask for the bill for your meal.

Cooked. *Cocida* (koh SEE dah).

Cup. *Copa* (KOH pah). When the word is used with wine as in copa de vino (KOH pah deh BEE noh) it means a glass of wine.

Eating Utensils. *Cubierto* (KOO bee YEHR toh). Use this word when you're missing a knife, fork, and spoon.

Economical Food. *Comida económica* (koh MEE dah eh koh NOH mee kah). Literally, it means economically priced food. You'll see this sign above restaurant doors that seek clients who want well-priced food. Often large families will dine at such places. Generally the food will be good, authentic Mexican fare, the portions ample, and the service polite if not quick. But the atmosphere is almost always plain; perhaps the restaurant will be furnished with metal tables and chairs, or located in the living room of the cook's home with plastic flowers dotting the plastic table coverings. Seldom disappointing in terms of quality of food for the price paid, such places, however, should be given a cursory review for cleanliness before settling in for a meal.

Fat. *Gordo* (GOHR doh). This word for fat refers to size. (See also *Grease/Grasa* below.)

Fork. *Tenedor* (teh neh DOHR).

Glass. *Vaso* (BAH soh). A vaso would be sized for drinking milk, water, beer, or a soft drink, etc.

Grease. *Grasa* (GRAH sah).

Greasy. *Grasiento* (grah see YEHN toh). You might want to tell the waiter that something is too greasy.

Homemade Food. *Comida casera* (koh MEE dah kah SEH rah).

Hot. *Caliente* (kah lee EN teh). Caliente is hot to the touch or from the flame. Spicy hot is *picante* (pee KAHN teh).

Ice. *Hielo* (YEH loh). (For precautions regarding ice consumption see also Menu Primer A to Z: *Hielo.*)

Knife. *Cuchillo* (koo CHEE yoh).

Medium. *Mediano* (meh dee YAH noh). This will be useful when sizing a pizza, bowl of soup, salad, etc.

Medium Well Done. *Medio turno* (MEH dee yoh TOOR noh).

Menu. *Carta* (KAHR tah).

Napkin. *Servilleta* (sehr bee YEH tah).

Pepper. *Pimienta* (pee mee YEN tah). This is the word for black table pepper.

Pinch. *Pizca* (PEEZ kah). A pinch of something such as salt, pepper, or an herb for flavoring. Salt and other condiments are sometimes set on the table in bowls (without spoons), from which you pinch the amount you want.

Prepared Spice Mixture. *Recado* (reh KAH doh). A recado is a mixture of spice ingredients ready to take home and cook. In markets recados are the ready-made pastes of adobo, achiote preparado, mole, etc. Spice is *especia* (ehs PEE see yah).

Purified. *Purificado* (pooh ree fee KAH doh).

Rare. *Poco cocido* (POH koh koh SEE doh).

Salty. *Salada* (sah LAH dah). Use this word to say the food is too salty.

Shish Kebab. *Pinchito* (peen CHEE toh) or *brochetta* (broh CHEH tah) are words for shish kebab.

Skinny or **Thin.** *Delgado* (dehl GAH doh). *Flaco* (FLAH koh) is another word for skinny.

Small. *Chica* (CHEE kah) or *pequeño* (peh KAIN yoh).

Spicy Hot. *Picante* (pee KAHN teh). Picante means spicy hot. To discover if a dish is picante ask, *"¿Es picante?"* (ehs pee KAHN teh). The waiter may reply, *"No es picante"* "It isn't hot" or *"Es picante"* "It's hot," with a great big nod. Or the reply may be *"No se pica"* (no seh PEE kah), meaning it won't burn you with its spicy taste. He might also say, *"Se pica un poco"* (seh PEE kah oon POH koh), meaning "It's a little spicy hot" or has a bite. *"No pica mucho"* (noh PEE kah MOO choh) means "It's not very hot."

Spoon. *Cuchara* (koo CHA rah).

Sugary or **Sweet.** *Azucarado* (ah soo kah RAH doh). If something is too sweet this word could be used.

Or employ it to say you want something very sweet or muy azucarado (mooh ee ah soo kah RAH doh).

Tablespoon. *Cucharada* (koo cha RAH dah).

Teaspoon. *Cucharadita* (koo cha rah DEE tah).

Toothpick. *Palillo* (pah LEE yoh).

Water. *Agua* (AHG wah). Purified water is agua purificado (AH waah poo ree fee KAH doh). (See also Menu Primer A to Z: *Hielo*.)

Watery. *Aguado* (ah WAH doh). You may want to tell the waiter that a drink, soup, or sauce, etc., is too watery.

Well Done. *Bien cocido* (bee YEHN koh SEE doh).

MARITA ADAIR admits sleuthing aromas in countless kitchens, bubbling kettles, and streetside eateries to unlock the secrets behind Mexico's wonderful cuisines. Her storehouse of Mexican-purchased chiles, mole, adobo, achiote preparado, and pipián grows after each of her numerous trips south of the border. She also confesses succumbing to numerous uncontrollable urges to create Mexican feasts while writing this book, and to cultivating her own crop of chiles to fuel the cooking furnace. She specializes in writing about Mexico and her award-winning work has appeared in numerous newspapers, magazines, and books.

· ▚ ·